PRAISE FOR *STORY. STYLE. BRAND.*

"Brand is storytelling and the emotional component that subliminally engages a customer, an employee, a partner, or a collaborator is core to the human condition. This is a powerful approach to strategically leveraging what is natural. An excellent read and powerful advice!"

Andy Cunningham
Bestselling Author, *Get to Aha!: Discover Your Positioning DNA and Dominate Your Competition*

"The secret's out! Janel's methodology has been my secret weapon for both large corporate events and personal engagements. Now, everyone can be inspired by her approach to building a personal brand through story and style."

Lynn Vojvodich
Member of the Board of Directors for Dell, Ford, and Booking Holdings; Advisor and Investor in Technology Companies; Former Tech Sector CMO

"Being a corporate leader or ambitious entrepreneur can pose distinct challenges for women who seek to find personal fulfillment as well as professional success. Janel Dyan understands. Her powerful book, *Story. Style. Brand.*, is an honest invitation to readers to rethink their own stories, discover their unique senses of style, and develop personal brands with confidence and ease. Janel believes, as I do, that meaning and story matter. This book is sure to strike a chord with business executives and owners on many levels."

Shilpa Shah
Co-Founder and CXO, Cuyana

"This book is one that all professional women should read as they consider the importance of their personal brands to their careers. Janel is an excellent, thoughtful and gracious partner to female executives looking to bring their best selves to work and to the stage — no matter what the size."

Shannon Brayton
Executive, Board Director, Investor

"At the root of Janel's many talents and accomplishments is an innate ability to relate to other people with clarity and compassion. It's that ability that's enabled her to change client's habits of self-perception and allow them to stand taller, prouder, and most of all, authentically before their audiences. And because she builds that from each person's own truth, the change she brings about endures and grows stronger over time. To see her bring this talent to the art of branding gives us hope for change in the way that companies relate to their employees and customers."

Todd Sieling and Tylor Sherman
Co-founders, Denim & Steel Interactive

"Janel Dyan has accomplished something remarkable — she has proven that when you live your life story, your style has the power to connect, inspire and engage. In my work with Janel, I've discovered that we can use the lessons of the JD Methodology to serve not just ourselves and our companies, but to go 'Beyond Us' to become a movement of women empowering, supporting and investing in other women. Janel challenges you to be the woman who remembers to look back, reach down, pull another woman up and give her the permission to be powerful in her own light. I have no doubt that this book and its extraordinary author will change countless lives, companies and careers."

Ebony Frelix Beckwith

EVP and Chief Philanthropy Officer at Salesforce; Board Member at Hamilton Families and Women's Funding Network

"What you wear should reflect who you are. In business today, personal style — what perhaps has been an afterthought — is fundamentally important. You will deliver your best work if you are your authentic self ... authentic in how you dress, what you say and what you do. For women taking the helm of powerful organizations, every decision — including how you carry yourself into the room or onto a stage — has the opportunity to support a strategy, drive home a story or connect with the people you're in business to serve. Never before have I seen a business book tackle this conversation as clearly and with such inspiration as Janel Dyan's *Story. Style. Brand.*"

Susan St. Ledger

President, Worldwide Field Operations, Splunk

"Janel Dyan is a woman who is driven to help others understand that style is what stands between personal story and professional brand. That what you wear is a reflection of authenticity and a means to start a conversation and establish a deeper connection. What women need and deserve today — in work and in life — are a platform for growth and a community to support them. I am fortunate to have Janel in my own personal community because she's the real deal — humble, open-minded, hard-working and generous. Readers of this book are sure to walk away not just inspired but feeling they have made a new friend."

Suzanne DiBianca
Executive Vice President, Corporate Relations and
Chief Impact Officer, Salesforce

"Eye-opening and a fresh take on women's unique position in the global e-commerce marketplace. Janel's insights and vivid stories are raw, vulnerable and empowering for women everywhere. She is a quietly confident powerhouse."

Jessica S. Eker
Senior Vice President, TransPerfect

"The key to Janel's approach to style is that she isn't actually helping you with fashion ... she's helping you express yourself to the world. As your story evolves, so should your brand. This book is for everyone as you navigate your career."

Elizabeth Walton Egan
Vice President, Marketing at Yext; *Forbes* 30 Under 30,
Marketing and Advertising

"Janel's approach to storytelling goes beyond delivering brand value — she empowers people to define, own and align their personal stories to lift others. She has been the secret force behind some of the most successful executives and now she is sharing her process. This is a must read."

Allie Cefalo

Communications Executive, San Francisco Bay Area

"Initial impressions are made quickly, and smart businesses will not only understand this, but will capitalize on the way that authenticity, transparency and vulnerability impact that decision. Janel Dyan makes the case for personal branding in her excellent new book, *Story. Style. Brand.* Use her wisdom to ensure your organization is maximizing your impact."

Cathy Fyock

Speaker and Author of *The Speaker Author: Sell More Books and Book More Speeches*

"An entertaining and vulnerable story of one woman's grit and her vision to help women and corporations control the conversation while establishing an emotional and authentic connection with others."

Sylvia Borek

Sales Executive and TedX Speaker

"Many will read this book and discover the JD Methodology and its relevant uses to their company and their brand, but these pages also hold Janel's spirit — her authenticity, drive, passion."

Joanne Choi

Independent Writing and Editing Professional, San Francisco Bay Area

"Women in the workplace have so much to balance that it can be a juggling act to keep it all going. Janel Dyan is a master juggler who approaches women leaders — through her work and through her book — with honesty, vulnerability and integrity. She understands the challenges of being a parent, a business owner and the daughter of a mother with chronic illness. I, too, am a parent, a business owner and my mom lives with Parkinson's Disease; as such, this book hit me on so many levels. But you don't have to have been through what Janel's been through to know that the pressures (and opportunities) of life and career for high-achieving women can leave you with emotions spread out like a garage sale. Those emotions are part of your story; your story informs your style; and your style can be the backbone of your brand. It's vital to embrace it all."

Brenna Nichols

Founder & Owner, Gifted for You, Chicago

"Janel Dyan reminds us that every step we take, in our clothes, our posture, and our demeanor, sends messages of our confidence Our authenticity. Our empowerment. Our value. I felt an immediate connection with Janel's message. Over the past several yers, I broke out of my "black suit, black pumps, blond hair" bonds and found a new way to be professional and personal. Now my wildly colored hair and fun shoes are a trademark, but never mar my ability to be taken seriously. Men and women both will find valuable takeaways from this book. It will challenge you 'look in the mirror' in a whole new way."

Michael Sherlock

Transformational Leader, "Shock Your Potential" Podcast Host, Speaker, and Author of *Tell Me More: How to Ask the Right Questions and Get the Most Out of Your Employees* and *Sales Mixology: Why the Most Potent Sales and Customer Experiences Follow a Recipe for Success*

STORY. STYLE. BRAND.

Why Corporate Results Are a Matter of Personal Style

JANEL DYAN

Story. Style. Brand. - Why Corporate Results are Often a Matter of Personal Style

By Janel Dyan

Published by Silver Tree Publishing, a division of
Silver Tree Communications, LLC (Kenosha, WI).
www.SilverTreePublishing.com

The author shares within this book stories and anecdotes with deep respect for those people mentioned. To the degree that it was possible, she also did so with their permission and/or understanding.

Editing by:
Stephanie Feger
Kate Colbert

Cover design and typesetting by:
Courtney Hudson

Cover photo photographer: Ana Vega

Cover photo model: Janel Dyan

First edition, November 2019

ISBN: 978-948238-21-2

Library of Congress Control Number: 2019914839

Created in the United States of America

DEDICATION

Mom,

You taught me that stories do matter,
clothes can inspire and being real is the only way to live.
You are the first brand I ever loved.

This is for you.

xx – j

TABLE OF CONTENTS

LETTER TO THE READER

My number one focus when I launched my company, Janel Dyan, Inc. (JD), was to be authentic and humble every step of the way, with an imperative that every decision must come from a place of truth, discovery and the drive to make other lives better. As you begin reading this book, you may be coming to the experience with preconceived notions about personal branding, about style or fashion, or about what you imagine it is that I do to help leaders tell their stories and to build or reinforce corporate brands through style. Know this: It isn't about the clothes you wear ... it's about the story you are sharing with the people in the room. It's about starting with the story, building in style to align with that story, and giving ourselves permission to be authentic in the expression of our personal and professional brands.

Building your brand is about envisioning who you want to be, where you want to be and what you want to be doing — even if it's not clear yet. We must start somewhere. Perhaps you're starting with this book. Thank you.

In the following pages, I attempt to practice what I preach by first inviting you into my story — by telling you about my life and where I've been. I think this matters because we, as human beings, matter. You see, whoever we are and wherever we find ourselves in our lives or careers, our unique individual story precedes any authentic sense of style we can ever develop. In turn, it is that story-inspired style that builds the brand — big or small, global or domestic, in any industry or sector or organizational culture. So, come with me back to the beginning, so you can learn how to apply the simple but powerful "Story. Style. Brand." approach and the JD Methodology to control the conversation in your own life, company and world.

Because here's the thing: Fashion choices have always communicated something to the world — about identity, values, community.

This is my story ... raw, honest and full of incredible women and men who have helped shape who I am today and inspired me to build a business that is driven to make a difference in the lives of people and in the success of businesses. It is my hope that you will realize that your story has the power to connect, your style has the ability to engage and your brand has the capacity to inspire.

Your style has the ability to engage and your brand has the capacity to inspire.

Not All Stages Involve a Platform and a Microphone

I've come to learn that not all "stages" involve a platform and a mic. Each day you wake up, you will likely find yourself preparing for a moment on a stage of some sorts — usually metaphorically, sometimes literally. Maybe you will be standing in front of your employer, pitching a new opportunity. Possibly, you will head in for a workplace interview for a job promotion. You could be required to lead (or co-lead) a large work project or be the spokesperson for your company's newest product launch. And, arguably just as important but many times overlooked, you may be standing on a curb or in your driveway, in the elementary school drop-off line or at a PTA meeting, just like I was when I first discovered I had a story to tell, a style to cultivate and a brand to share with the world. My most important audience was small but mighty — two kids watching my every move, learning from the steps I took and from those I opted not to take. Perhaps you can relate.

Whatever your "stage" may be, own it by owning your story first. Who do you want to be? What part of your life's story is holding you back? Why haven't you let go of it? Where do you want your life to take you? What would you do if the answer to each great opportunity was "yes?"

I wrote this book for individuals who have brands, reputations and careers, as well as for corporate leaders and organizations seeking fresh ways to think about how to leverage the "presence" of their leaders, particularly their female leaders. This is a conversation that matters, and few people are having it.

Style is the missing link between the story and the brand. We may not choose how the plot of our life unfolds, but we can choose whether we see a tragedy as a beginning or an end. We can choose how we stand up for what we believe in, when to accept the battles we have lost and those we choose to continue to fight. Most of all, we can use our stories for good, to turn around and lift up others and know that our clothes can live our stories ... for us, for our organizations, and Beyond Us well into the future if we choose to upcycle our fashion to friends.

As a woman entrepreneur, I've learned that the most important aspect of your brand is not always built upon the product or services that your business is creating. It's about you, your story and your vision. It's about believing that "no" means "not right now" and trusting that failure is inevitable — so fail forward, often and boldly. Give yourself permission to screw up. You will make mistakes. Every day. Remember, with each step you take, you get better, you get stronger. And that's what matters. It matters that you just keep going.

We all have a story, and our stories guide us in everything we do. They are unique and should be shared. Because stories have the power to change people's lives. Thank you for allowing me to share mine.

This book can be read any way you want. If you want to know the full story, turn the page. If you want to read it in sections, starting with sections that have topics or titles that matter most to you, go for it. Just jump in and enjoy.

xx – j

INTRODUCTION

It's often said that first impressions happen within the initial seven seconds of meeting someone. I disagree. In fact, I believe first impressions happen much sooner and within what I call "The First Three Steps." It is that unconscious gut decision that helps us decide if someone is trustworthy or threatening when they walk into a room, onto a stage, into the frame of a corporate video or even past us on the street. It is nearly impossible for us not to make these "snap" judgments about one another. It's how we're hardwired. It's in our DNA.

Trust is an emotional response, and storytelling is the most essential element in establishing it.

Trust is an emotional response, and storytelling is the most essential element in establishing it.

It is our ability to establish trust that matters most. For human nature shows that without the establishment of trust between each other, believing the truth will be an uphill battle.

How clients appear — including what they wear — is the first step and, arguably, the most critical step of the story they tell an audience.

The JD Methodology was developed on the belief that by understanding, embracing and capitalizing on our human behavior, we can use our DNA to our advantage. With the JD Methodology, it is possible to influence those natural human judgements to set us up for the success we deserve. With our First Three Steps, we can control the conversation, on every level, using sensory details, whether our audience realizes it or not.

Marketing, at its core, is simply about storytelling. It's the ability to take consumers on an emotional journey that can relate to their shopping behaviors — their needs and wants — while, at the same time, establishing trust in the products and services we sell.

The World's Most Powerful Consumer

Women are the most powerful consumers in today's global market. According to Bridget Brennan, author of the two books *Why She Buys: The New Strategy for Reaching the World's Most Powerful Consumers* and *Winning Her Business: How to Transform the Customer Experience for the World's Most Powerful Consumers*, approximately 70 to 80 percent of all purchases are either bought or heavily influenced by women.[1] Knowing this, I question why the majority of decision makers regarding the design, distribution, sales and marketing of most products and services are men, especially knowing that 91 percent of women feel that advertisers don't understand them.[2]

Therefore, to be successful with the most powerful consumers out there, a company must give their products and services a story

---

1 Bridget Brennan. *Why She Buys: The New Strategy for Reaching the World's Most Powerful Consumers*, Crown Business, 2011. Bridget Brennan. *Winning Her Business: How to Transform the Customer Experience for the World's Most Powerful Consumers*, HarperCollins Leadership, 2019.

2 *Ibid.*

that women can relate to. They must create a brand that women will buy from, advocate for and remain loyal to. Female consumers are the biggest influencers in the success of a company's return on investment.

"Women are a compass for how the market is changing," says Brennan. "... we must upgrade our customer experiences to stay relevant. In a consumer economy dominated by women, new skills are needed."[3]

> "Women are a compass for how the market is changing," says Brennan. "... we must upgrade our customer experiences to stay relevant. In a consumer economy dominated by women, new skills are needed."

The answer is in the ability to create an emotional connection between the information companies and organizations want to get across and the audience they are trying to reach. If it's known that snap decisions are happening and that women are the biggest consumer market, connection with them needs to happen in an instant. I've made it my job to help ensure those instant connections.

Women Selling to Women

Companies should adjust their marketing strategies to bridge this gap by investing in their women leadership. In addition to retention and motivation reasons, it's also important to realize that women are a company's most valuable asset in selling to the biggest global consumer — other women.

---

3 *Ibid.*

Investment in each female leader is essential for giving her confidence as she steps onto the stage (and into board meetings, sales pitches and other profitable engagements) because the story she is about to tell must be authentic, engaging and relatable. What she wears is critical to deliver this.

Section 1

IT ALL BEGINS WITH A STORY

"She remembered who she was, and the game changed."

- Lalah Delia

Behind the Scenes: Dreamforce 2018

It's showtime.

Electric energy emanates from the crowd. A powerful boost of "hell yeah" lets you know you are a part of it all. We, the Janel Dyan, Inc. (JD) team, are an integral piece. Backstage, the Dreamforce events team works like a well-oiled machine. It's apparent that they have spent the past nine months preparing for this one week, and even the veterans of the company are as pumped today as they were the first time. This team runs one of the biggest shows in the tech world with a cool calmness that sets the tone for the rest of us. With high and positive energy, their passion and belief in what they do is infectious.

The lights dim in the theater. A repetitious tune fades in from the speakers as 13 giant LED screens reveal a video that starts with one line: "Let's hear it for revolutions ..." The Dreamforce main keynote has begun. Shortly, Salesforce's Chairman and Co-CEO Marc Benioff will take the stage at the Moscone Center to welcome a packed room of 8,000 people (and millions more online).

Music pulses as chatter streams in from the attendees finding seats up front. You can feel the intensity in the air, and adrenaline builds with every song. They are all here to learn what Salesforce is launching and how to be a part of the next revolution of modern business.

"She's two minutes away." Her assistant's text pops up on my phone. "She" is the woman we're styling for this critical keynote and the JD team is ready for her in dressing room #2. Our job is to build a look that not only represents who she is but that also gives her instant credibility with her audience and the product she is presenting. Backstage, we transform these elite speakers in the near dark, as a constant mist spouts from the fabric steamer and one full-length mirror in the corner reflects the dim lighting. My tailor (or, as the team calls her, "the magician") pulls out her needle, thread and scissors. Each outfit for the stage has been steamed, tailored and reconstructed. Each is hanging with the appointed shoes underneath, awaiting its turn.

It is critical that we ensure the keynoter's next 20 minutes of time with us in the dressing room runs as calmly and smoothly as possible. This is her reprieve from the conference, giving her time to disconnect from the chaos and pressure. It's her chance to refuel. For some, being in our dressing room is their favorite part of the day. When the door closes, only the JD team can come in or out until she's ready. She can compose herself in this safe space.

For some, being in our dressing room is their favorite part of the day.

Standing in front of the mirror, she centers herself with her hands clasped and elbows out. My team surrounds her from every angle with iPhone flashlights in their hands. We review our punch list. Readjust the top. Check the hemlines. Look for stray threads.

From head to toe, we have everything covered. The "what if's" — like zipper pops, showing bra straps, heel blisters, sweat marks and Spanx lines — are of no worry for her. This outfit needs to be flawless. This is a performance. We know the stakes. She walks across the room to see the outfit from all angles. The knock on the door from the backstage crew comes, and an eager voice wafts through the door, asking if she is ready. It's time.

The backstage audio crew is on point, equipped with clipboards, schedules and headsets. "Check, check." "Mic feel, good?" "Okay, she's here and ready."

"Ready?" I ask her. With a deep breath and one last look in the mirror, we depart with high fives. It's a go.

I turn to the team to make sure they are on the same page. They know what I am thinking without my lips ever parting. "No mistakes." For some, this will be the first time anyone has seen her in this look. The anticipation at the unveiling builds with excitement and intrigue. Over the years, waiting to see what she wears has become an anticipated event by every team member backstage and the audience who are waiting for her.

As she steps out from the dressing room, the Dreamforce event staff are outside waiting. Their response is important to her. It's important to my team, too. This reveal is one of my favorite moments. "Wow, love it." "OMG, you look incredible." "That color dress, where did you find it?" "Those shoes ... I have to get a pair." I see her confidence build. My team sneaks glances of congrats and exhales a quick sigh of relief.

It's game time.

Standing at the threshold of the backstage and the main floor, I watch as she transforms herself with a powerful confidence. Her shoulders roll back. She shakes out her arms, takes a deep breath and clears her throat. She's ready.

Booming from the mic: "Next, to tell you more about the Salesforce Marketing Platform, I'd like to welcome ..." She walks into the light, commanding it to follow her onto the stage. Heads turn to catch a glimpse of her as the music plays and the audience cheers. A surge of pride and empowerment envelops me as she walks up and takes her first three steps onto the stage.

First step. She is authentic.

Second step. She exudes confidence.

Third step. She amplifies.

Her first three steps onto the stage are the most critical time to build trust with the audience. In fact, her success depends on it.

Over the next several minutes, all eyes are on her. Nothing matters more than her ability to control the message with the audience. Engaging the audience to listen to what she is presenting is the ultimate success. I watch from the back of the room, my eyes capturing every detail of the audience. I read their body language. The way they shift in their chairs, look up from their phones and sit up a bit straighter. The energy in the room is shifting and her message is being heard.

She's killin' it.

Quickly, I run backstage to join the JD team as they watch it live on the TV monitors. We are fixated on all social media platforms: Tweets, Instagram posts and the Dreamforce trailblazer community app that tracks every comment. Within seconds, the feedback starts to stream. Her assistant, who is sitting in the first few rows of the audience, is snapping pictures, posting on Twitter and Instagram, then texting me the images as our keynote speaker commands the stage. I share the photos with my team as they huddle around me.

She signs off and hands the mic back to Marc. He thanks her. The audience claps. Almost done ... she needs to nail those three steps as she descends the stairs from the stage.

Three, she was engaging.

Two, she was empowering.

One, she inspired others to follow her path.

When the main keynote is complete, the music starts back up and the audience begins to exit the room. That's my cue to head out to see the client. We share a quick hug and snap the annual post-keynote picture to commemorate that, for her, another Dreamforce is in the books. Then I'm headed backstage to join my team as we prepare for our next incredible client.

One keynote down, many more to go. I'll sleep next week.

After all the preparation, rehearsals, late nights, early mornings, fittings and pressure to execute flawless keynote looks, another Dreamforce comes to an end. Over the four days of the conference, JD worked around the clock to accommodate our clients' jam-packed calendars, style tweaks, site changes and last-minute needs.

During the past 22 days, the JD team worked with 12 incredible women. From building looks from their own closets, pulling pieces for on-site appointments and redesigning an entire week of ensembles, it was a massive feat. We tirelessly sourced pieces from all over the U.S., and when needed, Europe. Every item was needed within 24-48 hours and every item was delivered.

Our incredible team at Nordstrom in San Francisco worked day and night, sourcing pieces from Los Angeles, Dallas and New York. A dedicated crew helped assist each client with white-glove service and was on standby during Dreamforce, ready to fetch any last-minute needs from the store.

The Neiman Marcus crew opened their doors at 7:00 a.m. with coffee, treats and water. Curbside pick-ups and courier service to each private appointment was flawless. There were days when I would be building looks in a dressing room before the sun rose and walking out to go home after the sun had already set.

The stakes are high and there is little room for error, but the adrenaline is addictive, the team is incredible, and the women are inspiring. With the culmination of building more than 65 outfits and countless working hours, the JD team's success is measured in two-minute increments.

The success of JD was not the culmination of the past years of hard work. In fact, my vision to build a company began one summer day when I was three years old.

My mother told me she was going to die.

CHAPTER 1

A Childhood Interrupted

In the early spring of 1980, I was 3 and my mother Barbara was 33. She had just been diagnosed with a severe case of Systemic Lupus Erythematosus (SLE). SLE, more commonly known as lupus, is an autoimmune disease in which the immune system attacks its own tissues, causing widespread inflammation and tissue damage in the affected organs. SLE can affect the joints, skin, brain, lungs, kidneys and blood vessels. Though there is no cure for lupus, medical interventions and lifestyle changes can help control the disease.

In order to treat the disease and control its devastating effects on her body, doctors put my mom on an extremely high dose of Prednisone. Psychosis is a potential side effect. My mom spent the next four months going in and out of reality as doctors adjusted the medication dosage and managed her side effects. Each time the psychosis hit, my father Lonny would sit down with my brother Jonathan and me and calmly explain that she was having a "bad dream with her eyes open." He tried hard to be there for us during each episode, even moving to a new office that was blocks away from the house so that he could be close at any time.

When these episodes would come, how long they would last and what the "dream" would be was an unknown that we could never prepare for. Mom could quickly go from talking about homework and sports to watching hallucinated butterflies and chariots flying around the room, nervously running down the hall to her bedroom fearing that her jewelry had been stolen.

My mom tried hard to let us know when another "bad dream" was coming. Often, she'd say, "What is happening is because of the medicine and it will pass soon." A glaze would soon fall across her eyes and she would disappear. No matter how many times it would happen, I always believed she would be OK.

Until the day she wasn't.

Early that morning, with a toxic level of Prednisone in her system, my mom shifted into a full state of paranoid psychosis. Believing that her father was in grave danger, she stood in the middle of the street screaming the same thing over and over: "Help me! My father is going to die!" Paranoia often gave her extreme physical strength and it took my grandmother some time to calm her down, get her back inside and to call for help. My dad still remembers that call, for it was to be the beginning of an eight-year fight to save my mom's life.

The call went a little something like this ... "Barb is paranoid. We need to get her help. Jon and Janel are here. We need to get them out."

It is a memory that is forever etched into my mind. I was sitting at the kitchen table with my mom seated across from me. My maternal grandmother was behind us putting the dishes in the dishwasher, and Neil Diamond was singing "I Am, I Said" on the record player. Mom was creating lesson plans for a calligraphy class she was teaching in our home that evening when she quietly stopped and put her pen down. Calmly, she looked up, and I knew. Her eyes were glazing over again.

"Sweetie, I am not going to be myself. Try to remember that I am still Mommy."

I vividly remember my grandmother's face at that moment. Her eyes held a mother's alarm for her daughter and a protective softness for her granddaughter. Stoic, loving and always by my mother's side, my grandmother knew what was happening. She had served her country as a nurse in World War II and spent the next 30 years as an ER nurse while raising her family. Her strength and unwavering love for my mom was undeniable during these times, and I can't imagine what she must have been feeling as she watched her daughter struggle that day.

Moments later, I was sitting on my mom's lap with her arms holding me tight. I knew I was safe but the anxiety and fear in that room were powerful and intense. Mom told me how much she loved me, my brother, my dad and her family. This made sense to me because she told me the exact same thing every night before bed. However, as I stared down at her wedding rings laid out on our kitchen table — the two rings I had just watched her slide off her finger — what she said next changed my world.

"Janel, I am going to die now. I want you to have these rings." My heart skipped a beat in my chest. Everything went silent and I could feel my body being tugged by my grandmother as she begged my mom to let me go.

My brother suddenly appeared in the kitchen doorway. Two and a half years older than me, he has always been my biggest protector. He stared straight at me, his eyes filled with a combination of sadness, fear, love and loss. It was in that moment, with my eyes fixated on his, I believed for the first time that my mom could be right. She might die.

What felt like minutes later, my dad walked through the front door. As my mom's paranoia increased, so did my mom's fear of letting me go and it would take both my dad and my grandmother to pull me away. My neighbor was called over to help pack up some things so my brother and I could head off for another "sleepover" as we said goodbye to mom.

That evening, my mom was admitted into the closed community unit of the psych ward at a local hospital in San Jose. The plan was to try and get her paranoia and psychosis in check and to figure out how to get control of the lupus.

During the next six weeks, my mom would fight hard to get better and went through unimaginable treatment. During one drug-induced episode, my mom was strapped down to a table and left in a small room. Face down and unable to turn her head or move her arms and legs, she spent 24 hours alone. With severe claustrophobia, she continuously asked for help that never came. After two weeks in lockdown, two weeks in intermediate care and another two weeks on the general care hospital floor, my mom's lupus finally seemed to be under control, and she was able to come home.

Over the next two months, despite all efforts by her medical team and the promises of the medications that the team was trying valiantly to manage, Mom just wasn't getting better. She would go back into the hospital two more times, staying six weeks at a time. She would battle two rounds of pneumonia, fight off Steven Johnson Syndrome (a disease that affects the mucous membranes and skin) — which caused third-degree burns all over her entire body — and endure several bouts of thrush that left her with internal scarring in her esophagus and stomach, permanently damaging her vocal cords. She wasn't getting better; in fact, she was getting worse.

Exhausted, frustrated and feeling that time was running out, Dad knew that in order to save her, he had to enlist the leading experts in the field. He decided to take her to the one place we knew was pioneering research on lupus and other autoimmune diseases:

Stanford Hospital in Palo Alto. By the time my mom arrived at Stanford, a toxic cocktail of antibiotics had ravaged her brain and body. She had been pumped full of six different medications, four of which were given at near-lethal levels. In fact, doctors told my father that she was one of the most severe cases the team at Stanford had ever seen. Her chances of survival were slim, and she may not make it to the next morning.

My dad's greatest fear was losing the one woman he ever loved. At the age of 33, with two children under five and medical bills piling up, he lived with the very real possibility that not only could he lose his wife, but he could lose our home, our way of life and a sense of stability for his children. He would say goodbye that night and pray that she would wake up in the morning.

She did.

Living with Lupus

During the next eight years, life with Mom's lupus was unpredictable for our family. Mom went in and out of the hospital regularly, spending a minimum of six weeks at a time. A simple cold that would take the rest of the family a few days to recover from could make my mom septic and land her back in the ICU. During my first-grade year, mom stayed in the hospital for a total of 168 days.

We watched her constant exhaustion, dad carrying her around the house when she didn't have the strength to walk. We experienced her lying in bed with IVs and saw her hair fall out. We helped feed her when she couldn't move her joints and spent many afternoons sharing the stories of our day while she lay in bed. We saw her quietly suffer from the pain that struck at all hours of the day and night, and we brought her heating pads and ice packs to bring her some relief.

I knew that when I hugged my mom before heading out for school, it could be the last time I hugged her for weeks. I never knew, when I came home from school, if she would be there. I can't forget how quiet the house was when she was gone and the instant feeling of being lost as I walked to my parents' empty bedroom. The silence was heavy, the air smelled of Bengay, and her pajamas were always draped on the bed where she changed before taking off for her latest trip.

I remember ambulance sirens and lights on fire trucks outside our house. I remember my mom locking herself in the bathroom during fits of paranoia, fearing for her safety and believing that her loved ones were going to die. I remember Uncle Carl and my dad talking to her on the other side of the door, trying to calm her down so that she would open the door and allow them to help. I remember the neighbors standing outside their front doors with sadness or curiosity on their faces. I remember my grandparents, aunts, uncles and close friends would envelope my brother and me with kindness and love — offering us peace in our chaotic lives. Though the four of us couldn't always be together, I always held out hope that Mom would come back as soon as she could. She always would.

I remember the look in my mom's eyes when she would say "I'm going to be OK." The times when she left to go back to the hospital, I remember hearing her whisper, "No, Lonny. I'm fine. I just need to rest a bit." Yet, my dad knew. She was already riding another wave. Sometimes, I tried to give her my blankie to calm her, a part of me that she could take with her when she would head to the hospital. It often worked because I could tell from the expression on her face that she was going to fight not just for herself, but for my brother and me too.

I remember that visiting my mom in the hospital always came with a mixture of excitement and anxiety. What she looked like, the smell of the hospital and the beeping of the machines were overwhelming and there was always so much unknown. Would she have IVs in her arms? Would she be awake? Would she look sick? My dad never lied to us about her illness, but in retrospect, I realize that my parents only allowed us to visit when my mom appeared her best and had the energy to make our visit as fun as possible.

When she was strong enough, we would take her IV pole and ride the elevator to the first floor. After checking out all the options in the vending machine, we would create a picnic of Jell-O cups, chips, sandwiches and our treat of the day; M&M's were my favorite. We played Go Fish, rode up and down on her hospital bed, pushed each other around the unit in her wheelchair, and filled up on many overdue hugs and kisses.

Saying goodbye at the end of these visits was the hardest part. Jon and I would watch the clock when Dad gave us the five-minute warning and reality would set in. The toughest goodbyes were when mom's immune system was so vulnerable that she was unable to walk us out.

I remember her dressed in her white hospital robe, socks and overcoat; she would flash sign language for "I love you" from the small window of the entrance doors with the sweetest smile across her face. We walked backward, waving goodbye until we could no longer see her. Sometimes, Dad would let us run back for one more hug. When we knew that her room window faced the parking lot, we'd drive by for one last goodbye, honking twice as we drove off. My dad once explained: "We tried so hard to shield you from all of it, but you needed to see your mom. She needed to see you. You and your brother are the reason she fought every day to live."

Today, saying goodbye to my mom, dad, and brother holds the unspoken understanding between us that our time together will never be taken for granted. We still commemorate farewell with two quick honks, the "I love you" hand sign and a smile.

The Calm Within a Storm

I can honestly say that my childhood was wonderful. With both sides of my family living near us and my brother and me as the only grandchildren, there was always someone there to watch us from the sidelines, the bleachers or the audience. My uncles, aunts and grandparents never missed a single dance performance in 16 years; my parents were at every soccer, volleyball, baseball and basketball game. They never allowed lupus to be an excuse. They pushed me to excel in everything I took on and they demanded that I always give 110%. It wasn't that I had to get an "A" in every class but the expectation was that I always gave "A" effort. In fact, in 8th grade, I received a B+ in my geometry class. My grade was a direct reflection of my true effort. That summer, I repeated the course to ensure I got the learning I'd missed out on.

My grandmother sewed my ballet costumes and my 92-year-old great-great aunt was my math tutor, spending afternoons with me and a math book in her room at the senior living home. My parents were our coaches, teachers, volunteer parents and surrogate parents to our friends. My dad was the president of the Parent Teacher Association (PTA). We hosted the annual "All-American 4th of July" block parties with the neighborhood, which ended with a talent show on our front lawn. My mom went back to work as a substitute teacher at my middle school and then full-time at my high school. (I distinctly remember the times when she would end up being the substitute teacher for *my* class!) My dad was the most popular chaperone at dances. He even dressing up in a gorilla suit for a jungle-themed 8th grade dance! We had a batting cage in our backyard and walked to the local park for a pick-up game of soccer or a tennis match of boy vs girls.

The silver lining from the early years of lupus was the gift of family — a family that appreciated the time we had together and deeply loved each other. But mostly, the silver lining was the relationship I had with my brother Jonathan. We had to stick together during the rough times and learned how to know what each other was thinking simply with our eyes. My brother has always looked out for me, and it was because of this influence that I applied to the dance program and ended up following him to UCLA. It was because of him that I learned the gift of debate (trying to win arguments as we grew up) and it is because of him that I never felt that being a "girl" made me less of an athlete. He challenged me to keep up in sports, silently looked out for me in my academics, showed kindness when my heart was broken and was steadfast with his support when I needed it.

For a childhood like ours, we had no choice but to rely on each other. Jonathan is the only person in my life who really understands.

Learning the Power of Story

As I grew up, the full impact of my stories was sometimes hard for me to understand. Knowing when, how and who to share my personal history with was critical. I had to learn that my stories, at times, could be too emotional, too heavy or even off-putting for some. My stories, though I thought they weren't all that unique or difficult to share, were often beyond what others could understand or wanted to know. To this day, I still need to remind myself to be mindful of the stories I choose to share and that sometimes the audience just isn't ready or interested. For there is a fine line between when sharing a story can help two people to connect with each other and when sharing that story can take away the power of someone else's story.

Growing up with a childhood like mine impacts your perspective at a very young age. Experiences in my life would often be too difficult for others to relate to. When my friend would complain that her dad wasn't at her soccer game or that her mom was on her case about getting a bad grade on a test, I struggled to feel empathetic. My mom's health could change in an instant. *"You don't get it"* I'd say in my head as I listened to their stories. I would think, *"if they only knew."*

My mom was once admitted to the hospital because her lungs were hemorrhaging. She was in the ICU at Stanford where she shared a room with three other patients. We visited her that evening, had our vending machine treat, talked about homework and plans for the week and then said goodnight. The next morning when we arrived, all three patients sharing Mom's room were being carried out in body bags. Mom was the lone survivor.

This is a story that I rarely share. The first time I shared it with a classmate, the look on her face told me I'd gone too far for her comfort. Maybe some stories should be kept to myself.

For most young girls, autonomy and control are rare. There's not much that a little girl has control over. She has little to no say in when she can go to bed, what she will have for dinner, what clothes she can wear or even what hairstyle she can have. As a small child with a sick parent, you control even less. I never knew what I would be facing when I walked through the door.

Would my dad be sitting with my mother trying to figure out if she needed to get to a doctor? Would the neighbors be in the kitchen with casserole dishes for the week while my mother is away? Or would it be my mom, herself, with that glazed look in her eyes that I learned to recognize as a warning sign of trouble to come?

So, I had to learn how to read a room instantly. No matter who was in the room, I had to read their body language, the way they looked at me (or didn't) and decide in a split second what might happen in the next few minutes. Learning to adapt to my environment so that I could understand how to react was my greatest survival skill and what has turned out to be my superpower.

I had to learn how to read a room instantly.

Lessons from My Mother

My mother's outward appearance became incredibly important to her. While she was sick on the inside, she was always determined to look "healthy" and "normal" on the outside. Her strategically planned outfits allowed her to control the conversation — to project to the world not a dialogue of illness but of health and hope.

I watched Mom adhere to this fashion strategy and life philosophy over and over. She didn't select her best clothing to wear because she had events to attend. She did so because she hoped to look better than she had the last time the doctors had seen her. She taught me that by dressing how you want to feel, you can establish a story that starts the precise conversation you want to have. You transform into your most authentic and best self. Your visual style can make you instantly relatable and attract different treatment — simply because you are seen differently.

By dressing how you want to feel, you can establish a story that starts the precise conversation you want to have.

While my mother used her own clothes to control the conversation around her health, she taught me that I could use fashion and style to guide my own conversation in my own world. Most girls would universally agree that middle school is a rough time. Most just want to fit in, look cool, be accepted and, at times, not be seen at all. Acutely aware of this, my mother took me shopping. Nordstrom, Mervyn's, and the Gap were her classrooms. We would spend hours browsing, learning about the current trends, best fits for my body, and how to select pieces appropriate for my lifestyle and age. Because money was tight, when the time came to purchase, we would go to Goodwill. We'd start in affluent neighborhoods and would bring along our newfound knowledge from the department stores to use as a guide while we perused the crowded racks.

When I expressed embarrassment over the second-hand clothing, my mother simply paused, looked me in the eye, and said "Life isn't about fitting in as much as it's about standing out. You aren't the only girl that shops at Goodwill nor the only one that may be embarrassed shopping there. So, instead of fitting in, be seen. Start a trend and call it GW."

Eventually my embarrassment subsided, and I began to cherish those moments and lessons. We tried not to miss the local flea market the first Saturday of each month. With a donut and hot chocolate in hand, we would walk up and down until we saw every table. We were on the hunt for unique pieces of clothing or accessories.

I became more comfortable with what pieces I had, how they stood out and what stories they told about me each day.

When my mom coordinated the annual neighborhood "Back to School Block Clothing Swap," I was excited to be able to share my outgrown pieces with the younger girls. I couldn't wait to take home pieces from the older girls that I could make my own. My mom would lay out black plastic bags on our front yard, and all the kids would walk over with their arms full of clothes that no longer fit, or ones they wanted to trade with each other, and put them onto the bags. I learned that just by switching up my wardrobe with my neighbors and friends made wearing used clothes new and cool.

I vividly remember taking home "Hilary's skirt." Hilary was my neighbor, was a year older than me and was someone I looked up to for so many reasons. When I wore that skirt to school, it made me feel invincible. At the same time, it was such a rewarding feeling to be at school and see Jessie wear the clothes I had swapped. My stories and memories when I wore those pieces would come back in my mind and I'd smile. Whether it was my birthday dress from last year or my most favorite Banana Republic graphic T-shirt, there was something so viscerally empowering in knowing that a simple act of sharing could make an impact on someone else.

My mother taught me that it was important to be honest about my life and taught me how to build my style around it. She taught me that it doesn't matter where I shop, what label I wear or how much it costs. She taught me that what matters most is me.

It doesn't matter where I shop, what label I wear or how much it costs ... what matters most is me.

Me, who has the power to start a trend and not follow one. Me, who can be proudly share my story. Me, who can empower others to share their stories. Me, who can stop worrying about fitting in and strive to be seen. And, me, who can stand alone and help others to stand with me.

No matter what was g oing on with my mom or how many trips to the hospital we had to make, the house was always filled with music, dancing and singing. Whether it was my mom waking us up to the tune of "Reveille" on the piano or my dad flipping on our bedroom lights while singing Bing Crosby's "When the Red Red Robin Comes Bob Bob Bobbin Along," there was always a massive blanket of love, laughter and pure joy that was wrapped around our home.

I cherish the memories of pushing all the furniture to the walls to put on talent shows in the living room with my friends. I loved listening to the Bee Gees 8-track with my dad, singing Lionel Richie alongside the piano with my mom, spending hours in front of the boom box making mix tapes of recorded songs from the radio with my brother and hosting impromptu dance parties in the kitchen with my grandparents.

My teen years were a mixture of dance and team sports. I grew up with a room full of pink, leotards and tights and a ballet barre that my uncle built, and my team sports pictures on the wall. There was a batting cage in the backyard, shin guards thrown at the front door and pointe shoes laying on my bedroom floor. I spent hours both practicing my porta bras and battement dégagés and in the front yard playing catch with my dad or at the soccer practice field taking shots on goal.

The Lights of the Stage

I started my first ballet class six months after my mom was diagnosed with lupus and, from the start, dancing allowed me to create any story I wanted. It was my therapy, a chance to escape — if just for a few hours a day — and get caught up in another world.

"Dance can elevate our human experience beyond the words."

- Judith Jamison, Artistic Direction Emerita from Alvin Alley American Dance Theater

I loved the preparation for class — the ballet shoes, tights and leotards. I loved watching the older girls warm up while I was waiting for my class to start and dreaming that someday I would be dancing en pointe. But it wasn't until my first dance recital that I knew I had found a safe place to tell my story: the stage.

I spent the next 16 years dancing, and many of my life lessons — and those that I now incorporate into the professional work that I do — were learned in those dance classes and on the stage.

- If you make a mistake, pretend it didn't happen. Just keep dancing.
- Your performance tells a story without you ever saying a word.
- If the costume isn't right, it'll distract from the experience you are creating for the audience.

Dance was my way of getting lost in the pursuit of perfection in an art that could never be perfect. It was a physical escape full of music, movement and freedom.

From middle school through high school, I worked hard to afford dance classes five days a week. With only a partial scholarship, my tuition was adding up. So, when I was in sixth grade, I began working as a teacher's assistant. I started by working a handful of evenings each week, helping younger girls with their form and technique. I found that I not only loved to dance, I loved the whole production — creating stories through music, movement and, of course, beautiful costumes. By the end of high school, I was assisting with the choreography of dances for a studio of more than 150 students.

In my last two years, I was exposed to all the details of what made a good performance great. Costumes had to be tacked in the right location for movement and to hide any undergarments. I had to be ready in the wings to solve any problem, managing a backstage team and executing a flawless production. More importantly, I learned that by teaching others the art of telling a story, I gave the gift of empowerment. To watch this transformation with each of my students was an honor. When they found the freedom to be themselves, to build their confidence to command the stage while engaging with their audience, there was nothing more exhilarating. It was during those few minutes, when the light was on them, that all the hard work was worth it.

My drive to excel was also brought to the soccer field, basketball court and volleyball court. It was common for me to go to practice after school, then to dance class and then have my dad jump on his bike to cycle next to me as I ran three miles in the dark. Homework started at 10:00 p.m. and maintaining a 4.0 GPA was expected.

I would end up dancing my way to UCLA and earning a spot in their nationally ranked dance department, graduating with honors in 1999 with a history degree. That same year, I eagerly entered corporate America during the first dot-com boom. It would be in my early working years that my childhood experiences would play out to my benefit.

I would take the lessons my mother had taught me, the elevated expectations in school, sports and dance, my well-honed ability to succeed during times of chaos and the non-stop pace of my childhood and put them to new use. Those skills and habits would take my career to the next level.

And then bring it to a sudden stop.

CHAPTER 2

Career and Motherhood

I was 22 years old when I started my career in corporate America, working in Santa Monica, California, at eCompanies, LLC. A business incubator and venture capital fund for developing Internet companies, eCompanies helped start-ups get off the ground by providing services such as mentoring, funding and office space. Once a company was big enough and ready to go out on their own, they would then move out and another start-up would move in. The pace was fast and the exposure for me was massive.

Hired to support the CTO as his executive assistant, I was fortunate to have a boss who provided as much opportunity to learn as possible. I managed his travel, expenses and calendar, but he also gave me a window into the entire workings of the business. He gave me special projects outside my required duties and let me explore other parts of the organization.

I learned about start-ups, funding and acquisitions. I learned about growth strategies, operating plans, marketing budgets, sales models, product roadmaps, hiring practices and emerging technologies. I watched developers build and de-bug apps. I saw how organizations measured their success with data.

After a year, my drive and curiosity landed me at one of the incubated start-ups. I joined JAMDAT, an early entrant in the mobile gaming industry. I was brought into the operations team to help with human resources but, like all fast-paced startups, I quickly took on multiple positions based on need. I learned how to adapt quickly, moving from one set of duties to another. That's what I loved about it. From organizing the holiday party and offsite meetings to managing the office and helping with market research projects, I gained valuable early-stage operating experience. I even worked with the development team to help conduct quality assurance (QA) on games like Bejeweled and Tetris.

But from the start, I was most fascinated with the "human factor," understanding what motivates employees, how to recruit for the right cultural fit and ways to grow employees professionally. I spent late nights reading about how to grow a young company; attended courses and earned multiple certifications, and worked hard to establish, write and implement several organizational processes and procedures.

My drive was intense. I networked, found mentors, asked for extra projects, created my own projects and, at times, was brought into strategic meetings with the executive team. I had no fear of failing or making mistakes. Instead, what I feared most was that I wouldn't be allowed to grow at my own pace because of my age and how I was perceived.

Don't get me wrong ... I knew I had limited experience. But in an environment of high growth and a flat organizational structure, everyone worked long hours to get shit done and I didn't put limits on myself. At times, I wanted to be taken more seriously, especially because I knew that I was such an asset to the company. I also knew that the level of respect was often associated with a job title.

Whether it's true or not, there was a difference in *my* mind about how the world perceives an administrator vs. a manager vs. a director vs.

a vice president. I had gone above and beyond what I was hired to do and, yet, when I would ask for a job title change — one that would align with the responsibilities I either had or felt I could take on — I was met with resistance.

Like many start-ups, the office attire was casual. Most employees dressed in jeans, sneakers and a T-shirt. It wasn't always easy to spot an executive walking around, which, in many ways, was a great equalizer for the employees. Given that I was a few years out from college, my wardrobe fit in perfectly with the status quo. But after months of working long hours, taking on more responsibilities and being denied with my promotion request, I had an "aha" moment.

The only person who was holding me back was me. If I wanted to be seen as a strategic asset to the company, I had to believe that I was and dress for the job I knew I deserved.

The only person who was holding me back was me. If I wanted to be seen as a strategic asset to the company, I had to believe that I was and dress for the job I knew I deserved.

I went to Banana Republic and picked up a new wardrobe to fit the person I wanted to be. The next day I walked into the office with black trousers, a light blue button-down shirt, heels and my long blonde hair thrown back in a ponytail. I felt so confident. Just like my mom taught me, I dressed the way I wanted to be seen and the way I wanted to feel.

As I entered the lobby, one of the executives walking to a meeting suddenly stopped and looked up. "Are you interviewing for a job? You aren't leaving, are you?" Within my First Three Steps, I had changed my story by changing what I wore, and, in that instant, I changed the conversation. I had just created my first corporate brand, and my career took off.

> Within my First Three Steps, I had changed my story by changing what I wore, and, in that instant, I changed the conversation.

I got the title, felt respected and took over all of human resources for the company.

New York Bound

Six months after my husband Dave and I got married, we found out that my father-in-law's cancer had returned. The prognosis wasn't what we hoped to hear, and we decided to relocate to New York from California to spend as much time as we could get with him. At this point, I didn't know Dave's family very well but, upon hearing this news, I felt an urgency to learn as many stories as I could.

We would drive Upstate on the weekends to spend time with his father and family and attend doctors' appointments in Connecticut. While Dave worked back in the city, I would often sleep over during the week, supporting his mother with whatever was needed and spend nights listening to both his parents talk about generations past. I had a deep need to absorb as much history as I could. It was important to me that I learn as many stories as I could about my father-in-law ... just in case my future children might not be able to spend time with him.

Splitting my time between family and a career was a tough balance. To build up my network and continue to pay the bills, I started out working for a temp agency as a recruiter. It soon became clear to me that my California look wasn't aligning well with the New York corporate style. Skirt suits, pant suits, boots and wool coats were staple items that couldn't be found in my closet. A quick trip to several stores in Columbus Circle led me to my first "big" purchase of a Theory black wool pant suit, several J. Crew cardigans and my first pair of Sorel "Cate the Great" winter boots.

I learned that during the winter, work heels or flats are kept under your desk to change into after walking along the wet streets of the city. I learned that during the snowstorms, it didn't matter what your coat looked like — as long as you could cover your entire body and even your face. I learned that in the summer, keeping a sweater in your office was important because the hot and humid temperature outside greatly differed from the cold air-conditioned office you would work in. With my wardrobe updated and aligned to a New York professional brand, I landed a consulting job in the city and soon found success.

While standing on the corner of 61st and Columbus, I answered the call from Dave.

"The doctors said there is nothing more we can do for Dad."

Everything stopped. I was juggling both family and work but, in that instant, what I needed to do became clear. Our time here is short and I had to re-prioritize what mattered most. I decided that family should come first, and I resigned from my job.

Over the next few months, I spent most of my time Upstate, providing as much support as I could for his father and mother. It was a situation that I felt most comfortable in: an environment of nurses, medicine, hosting dinners for the neighbors, wheelchairs, IVs, long walks with Dave's mother and hospice care. Yet, as I have told many of my friends, spending that time with Dave's father was a great gift. I often think that he gave me more than I gave him. We talked about his childhood, his businesses and his children. He loved to listen to the rain, wore a collared shirt every day and held business meetings laying on the couch in his living room.

All this time spent together with Dave's family brought up conversations about starting our own family. Though I didn't realize it then, when John passed away, I was already pregnant. While we took some time to look for homes outside of New York City, deep down I knew that I always wanted to raise our children near my parents — not only for the support we would have, but also for the comfort of being just 20 minutes away from both their house and the Stanford Hospital.

So, without hesitation, I put a pause on my career to be a stay-at-home mom - something that I had always wanted to be.

Motherhood: My Greatest Achievement and Biggest Sacrifice

Motherhood, like life, can't be perfectly planned. When I was 27 weeks pregnant, I went into early labor and spent the rest of my pregnancy on bedrest. I fought hard to delay the birth. I was hooked up to IVs that tried to hold back my contractions and prevent infections. Each day, my mom would stay with me and, together, we played the same games we had played when she was sick. We would laugh and make jokes when the updates on the pregnancy weren't positive. It was a surreal experience for me. I was at Stanford Hospital and I was in the bed this time. Mom wasn't.

Our first son, JJ, was born at 33 weeks and one day. He was almost seven weeks early. He was immediately rushed to the Neonatal Intensive Care Unit (NICU) with my husband as I laid there feeling as if it were unfair. This wasn't the way I thought becoming a mother would play out. I had tried so desperately to keep him inside for so many weeks, but my body failed me, and it failed my son. My heart broke for what JJ would have to go through in the coming weeks. I didn't know what to expect for him and for us, and I felt the loss of control acutely.

Once our son was stabilized, I was wheeled into the NICU to hold him. He was in an incubator with IVs in his arm, a feeding tube, oxygen in his nose and the constant beat of his vitals in the background. I gently put my arms through the access holes in the incubator to place my hand on his body to rub his back. He was beautiful, and I was a mom. The deep instinct to protect my child kicked in. I remember turning to my mom and quietly asking, "Why me, Mom? What did I do wrong?"

"Look around you, Janel," she said.

I shifted my gaze from her face to finally take notice of what was going on around me. Five teeny babies were not just hooked up to IVs but were being kept alive by machines. A little girl's kidneys weren't working. A set of twins unable to breathe without assistance were surrounded by nurses and a mother, watching as doctors prepped the babies for heart surgery. Talk about perspective — just has mom had done during her bouts with lupus, she reminded me at a critical moment in my life to find hope and to have empathy for others.

"It could always be worse. You have a healthy boy who just need lots of hugs and time to grow," she said.

Over the next month, I spent every minute from 7:00 a.m. until 8:00 p.m. with him. Then I'd go home to get some rest while my husband or parents would come stay for the "night shift." JJ was held as much as we were allowed to hold him. From bradycardia, jaundice, feeding tubes and IVs in his arms, feet and head, his journey into the world wasn't one that I had hoped for, but it was one full of silver linings.

The nurses at Stanford's NICU were beyond incredible. They showed such love of my son, kindness to our family, support to me and Dave during the scariest of times, taught me how to handle the world of breastfeeding and pumping, and otherwise guided us through the early days of taking care of a newborn. It was a gift in knowing that when he was healthy enough to go home, I had some idea of what I was doing.

After 31 days, we took JJ home.

People don't talk much about what happens after you take your baby home from the NICU, but they should. My world became hyper-sensitive and I was overwhelmed. From the start, I felt more comfortable in the intensive care unit than I did at home. At Stanford, JJ's entire existence was based on numbers:

- Is he gaining enough weight?
- Can he drink on his own or how much milk did he take?
- Can he sleep without oxygen and for how long?

They don't tell you that, after spending days and nights reading the monitors for the blood oxygen levels or checking to make sure his heart rate was stable or ensuring that he was getting enough food via his feeding tube, you'll come to rely on those machine and metrics and the healthcare professionals just an arm's length away. When you go home and walk into the silence of a home, it's not only strange but scary. We became accustomed to, if not comforted by, the beeping, the lights and the alarms. If JJ started to cry and I couldn't comfort him, there was no nurse to help me or to take over.

Motherhood, especially the first time, is all about survival. It is a monumental transition that only experience can teach you how to handle. Babies aren't born with a "how to" manual. Learning to interpret their cries and gurgles, their sleep patterns or lack thereof, and knowing how much milk is enough for them is exhausting. Being a preemie baby, JJ had acid reflux and was unable to lie down without spitting up his milk. So, we spent the first five months sitting up and holding him through the night.

Motherhood, especially the first time, is all about survival.

Every two hours, I would pump on one side while he slept on the other side of my chest. Then once done, I would place the bottle between my legs to keep it warm until he woke up for another feeding. I've told many women that the worst form of torture for me was the lack of sleep. Here I was, tethered to a little life who I desperately loved beyond anything I could have ever imagined and, yet, all I could dream of was getting the chance to dream. I was up at all hours either with JJ or worrying about him while he slept.

The result for me was a new kind of existence — many nights at home, feeling extremely isolated and lonely (even if people were around) and, at times, absolutely full of anxiety.

- Is he drinking enough?
- Is he getting enough sleep?
- Am I starting a bad habit by holding him too long?
- Am I being a bad mom if he cries at all?
- Am I a failure if he can't breastfeed?
- Is it wrong to cry over him while he sleeps as the searing pain of mastitis hits me hard?

People say that, in times of transition, it's common to feel angry, depressed, confused, lost, guilty. It's part of your process, I was told. But over the first few months, those feelings weren't going away.

I remember dreading the nighttime because the night feedings could be so lonely and exhausting. I remember jumping in the shower so I could cry for no reason. I remember being so paralyzed by the fear of JJ crying that I struggled to put him in the car seat or even walk the eight blocks to my local Starbucks. I lost the desire to eat healthy, make new mom friends or answer phone calls from old friends. And I began to resent Dave because he "got to leave and go back to the corporate world." Lucky him. Yet, I held it together reasonably well until one evening, when I fully lost it. I was lying flat on my back in the middle of the kitchen and hysterically laughing/crying while saying that I was a "pencil." Dave looked at me and realized I needed help.

Postpartum depression snuck up on me. Every time I told my doctor that I was having feelings of sadness, anxiety, guilt or anger, I was told that "this is normal" and "it will pass." But it didn't. Getting into therapy and accepting medication was the best decision I made for myself. I began to feel better immediately. I found joy in the little things again, I was able to handle the stresses of motherhood, I stopped feeling guilty all the time, and I finally enjoyed my time with JJ and Dave. In time, I found other moms who had struggles like mine and established great friendships.

I loved being a mother, yet I had no clue what I was doing or who I was if JJ wasn't with me.

Identity Crisis, Humility and Acceptance

Motherhood has no defined career path. There are no set expectations of what makes a good mother. I wasn't a consultant anymore with projects and definitive deliverables. My job reviews wouldn't result in a promotion or increased income. Eventually, I recognized that back-to-school nights, report cards and parent feedback meetings were my job reviews. My office was my home. My home was my home. My most important project to manage would take 18 years (if not a lifetime) to complete.

Motherhood has no defined career path.

Pregnancy played on my insecurities and I lost my body for the first time. I gained 80 pounds in 33 weeks. Each month, the scale would confirm I had gained another 10 pounds. My body was expanding quickly, and I felt out of control.

Most of my life, I struggled to accept my body. During my junior year in high school, I had developed an eating disorder. It was hard to attend dance class, see your reflection in the mirror, and not then compare every line and curve to those of the other girls. It was a highly competitive environment. The dancers would be ranked twice a year. Placing top in the studio was the only outcome I would accept.

When I entered the UCLA dance program, I was told that I would "jump higher" if I could lose "a few pounds" as well. Standing at 5'8", my height made it difficult for a male counterpart to perform a duet that required him to lift me, as I typically would be taller than him. My body was slender, yet I felt huge.

Fast-forward to motherhood, and my struggle with body image was back, with a vengeance. After JJ was born, I felt awful when I looked in the mirror. I hated what I saw. I lost my figure, my control and my self-esteem. The extra skin, the thicker waist, the stretch marks and a bra size that was in the triple letters made me uncomfortable. Each morning, opening the closet to get dressed was depressing. Staring at all the clothes I could no longer fit in, I found that all the clothes of my past life just reinforced what I thought I had lost. So, I hid myself behind what I wore. Oversized T-shirts, boyfriend jeans, Dave's hoodies, and sweatpants were my go-to looks.

There was one gift from this emotional ordeal: a deep sense of humility. For the first time, I would experience what it was like to carry extra weight in this society. People treated me differently. Designer clothes weren't available in larger sizes and I felt judged when I sat down to eat a meal. There was a constant voice in my head, telling me to lift my pants up or pull my shirt down so that I covered any "muffin top" or hid any "sneak peaks" of my underwear.

Over the next few years, the postpartum depression began to fade and, with the addition of another son, Evan, we had become a family of four. I settled into life at home, took on a few part-time hobbies, and finally found a great community of friends and a network of support. But like anything in life, change happens when you least expect it.

Christmas in Chicago

In December 2011, my husband and I moved to a suburb of Chicago's North Shore. He had been given an incredible career opportunity to open a regional office for his company. Though neither of us had lived in the area — or ever imagined we would — it was too good to pass up.

Arriving two weeks before Christmas, I quickly learned just how unprepared I was to live in the Midwest. Unpacking the moving truck while wearing my Rainbow flip flops and a hoodie in 34-degree weather, it became quite clear that what I needed to wear would not be fashion-focused. My style (and survival!) in the bitter cold needed to shift. Function, not fashion, was top priority.

As I did in New York, I learned to wake up with the weather report on the news and to look out my bedroom window to see what people were wearing while walking by. Though I had lived through several snow seasons back East, nothing can compare to what it is like living through an artic freeze three blocks away from Lake Michigan. I had to learn how to drive in the snow, how to dress the boys for sub-zero temperatures and how to accept that outdoor play would still happen in the winter ... until the temps dropped below 10 degrees. I watched other moms at school drop-off to understand what clothing I needed to stay warm and invested in full-length down jackets, thermal layers, wool scarfs and incredibly expensive mittens.

And with the extreme weather that we were now living in, learning to manage my Raynaud's Syndrome (a rare disorder that causes the blood vessels to narrow when cold or under stress) became hard. Simply walking a long driveway would make my fingers and toes lose circulation, turn them white and leave them numb for hours. And now, because every beautiful North Shore home had a "no shoes in the house" rule, there had to be a way to keep my limbs warm and have style. So, I upped my sock game. No-show socks were my flats, and polka dots and stripes became my "pop of color." I had socks in the console of my car, socks in my handbags and, at times, would even find that I'd left socks in the pockets of my winter coats.

Women to Lean On

Moving to Chicago gave me another chance to rewrite, edit and share my story. No one knew my mom or her illness; they didn't know about my career in Los Angeles or New York; and they didn't know about my postpartum and struggles as a mom.

But it took time to find my support network of other moms who I could relate to — moms who I could share my real self with, moms who would be the right audience for my stories. In the beginning, it was about survival to figure out the town I was now calling home. "Where is the grocery store?" "What are the best winter boots to buy the boys?" "What service can I call for plowing the snow from my driveway?" But then I realized that these survival questions provided me with the easiest way to break the ice and let neighbors and others know that I was new to the area.

Given that we had moved two weeks before Christmas, trying to set up playdates took some time. So, it was in January that the boys began to meet new friends. With the weather dropping down into the single digits, we spent many new playdates inside the homes of other local families. And as much as their hospitality was beyond kind, I felt like I was dating all over again. I was the new mom in town and some people just wanted to know my "story" — not the real me. They sought the story of what my husband did, why we moved here or what I thought about the newest gadgets designed to get our littles to eat more during dinners.

By this time, JJ was 5 ½ and Evan was 3. I met Sara, my first real "Chicago friend," waiting outside the kindergarten classroom, there to pick up JJ. Sara would eventually introduce me to Lynn and then to Cindy. Everything clicked over dinner and a movie. Not only had I found three incredible friends, our husbands all became friends too. The Fab Four, I liked to call us ladies, were inseparable. We were all moms who didn't have parents near us, so we leaned on each other. A lot. We were an emotional support system, true friends and moms who liked to have fun. We had similar parenting styles that we could learn from. There was a deep respect for who we were, not just as mothers, but as women who also happened to be in the trenches of motherhood.

We looked after each other's children as if they were our own and were always there to help, no matter what. With 10 children among us, ranging from ages three to eight, we bonded over impromptu dance parties in Lynn's kitchen, obstacle courses in my home, ice skating on Sara's backyard ice rink and backyard summer pizza dinners at Cindy's.

These women became the sisters I never had. We would share clothes when needed, help get someone prepped before an event and, often, would give what we had so that they could enjoy a new style. There wasn't a competition but a sense of pride that we could help each other. It would be a gift that I would need one night in the fall of 2011.

Not Just a "Plus One"

As Dave's career advanced over the years, I became a "plus one" at corporate events, sales trips, client dinners and company holiday parties. Being my husband's dinner date for business occasions was a part that I was happy to play and eventually would look forward to. It was also, when the boys were little, a chance for me to have an adult conversation.

Even with all the prep in the world, the early years were awkward for me. I felt lonely standing quietly in a group listening, nodding and, at times, not understanding the content of the conversation. I had been out of work so long that I began to feel like I had nothing valuable to add to a conversation. I felt myself losing my voice. "What do you do?" was a cringe-worthy question I heard too often. It was not because my answer, "stay-at-home mom," was one I wasn't proud of — even loved to be — but that it was typically received with a pause, a change of subject and an underlining tone. And unless the conversation was about children, I would have nothing to add. "Let's get the ladies together for drinks," felt demeaning and dismissive when I struggled to add any personal market experience to the conversation. It soon became clear that if I walked away, no one would notice.

So, to make me as comfortable as possible, Dave and I established a plan in Chicago that would help me to prepare for each event. I began to study up about the people we were likely to meet at each event and glean a quick backstory on each of the attendees. I sought to know and remember the position they were in, the office they were working out of, a big sales deal they had just closed, what company or college they had just come from, who their "plus one" was and any personal stories about them that might overlap with my own interests or experiences. It was invaluable and key to help keep the conversations flowing.

What I wore was also important. I started researching ahead of time, calling other women I knew who were attending, searching online to see what the location looked like so that I could have a better idea of what "appropriate" attire (like "business casual" or "cocktails on the beach") actually meant for an executive's wife.

The most important aspect of these events for me, and what I treasure the most, was the ability to spend time with Dave's direct sales team *and* their "plus ones." Their stories, experiences and feedback on how things were going at work was fascinating. As I spent time with each member of his sales team, I truly got to know them. It is my belief that when you are in a position of the "plus one" for an executive, the time you spend with his or her team is a way of showing respect for what they do. For, if it wasn't for their hard work and Dave's leadership, I wouldn't be attending the event in the first place. I tried never to lose my gratitude and perspective.

A few years back, after more than 10 years of these events together, Dave and I decided to switch things up. Always fascinated with the "human factor" of a company and the keen ability to read a room, I wanted to be my husband's sounding board. So, on a bet, we decided to turn Dave's next event into a fun and productive test of my skills. Instead of getting a preview of all the key attendees this time, I decided I wanted to go in blind. No prep. No back stories. Dave would simply introduce me, and I took it from there.

If one of Dave's colleagues was accompanied by a "plus one," I would always engage them in the conversation. Their name might not have been on the invitation or the payroll, but they also had a voice and I wanted to hear it. Their combined story, the story of the two of them, helped me understand more of a 360-degree view of each of them, especially the employee. Let's face it, who you bring to a company event says a lot about you. And as we all know, first impressions mattered too, so what each person wore was an essential element for me. It wasn't about the designer they chose but about how they wore it, what part of the outfit they chose to bring up in conversation and the way their wardrobe choices aligned to their story. If the outfit didn't match their story, I would take a theoretical step back and ask myself *why* and then take on the challenge of finding the answer.

Without even realizing it, I became Dave's "secret weapon" at business events and I began to realize that my superpower was truly a gift — a gift that, as it came to life, energized me. The stories we shared, and those I merely listened to, empowered me. Being a "plus one" now gave me a purpose to truly connect with others — to read them, listen to the questions they asked and be able to share with Dave who they were ... who they *truly* were at the heart of it all.

On the ride home, with compassion, gut instinct, understanding of Dave's leadership style and the company they were working for, I would share my thoughts with Dave about what I believed motivated his team, what mattered most to them, whether they could thrive long-term in the corporate culture and how to lead them.

I then focused on each individual employee and the degree to which they appeared authentic in the way they shared their story — sometimes successfully and sometimes struggling to be so "real." Each employee had a story to tell. So, I started with their story, built in their style and shared what I believed their professional brand was. Nine out of ten times, I nailed it. And I still do.

Looking back at these past 15+ years, I realize I have grown just as much as he has. Unbeknownst to me, with every conversation that I couldn't "participate" in, I had been absorbing. With every discussion of struggles with company culture, sales pipeline, CRM implementation, enablement processes and strategic growth plans, I learned something vital that would become a huge asset when I launched my own company. And the relationships that I built over the years would be with people who became my biggest set of mentors and a truly supportive, powerful network. I cared about them and they cared about me, and no one was keeping score about who was a corporate VIP and who came into the conversation initially as someone's spouse, date or guest at a social gathering.

Now, when talk about Janel Dyan with these very same people — when I explain the services I provide and listen to their feedback — I learn invaluable lessons. Many of these friends and alliances had started a business of their own at one time, found great ways to handle rejection from clients and had navigated through tactical aspects like trademarks, contracts and the latest CRM software. They might work inside a large corporation with a boss and pecking order, but they were entrepreneurial at heart, and I connected with them on so many levels.

It's interesting for me to look back on the evolution of these relationships and of my attitude and strategy when it came to accompanying my husband to business events. I wasn't just somebody's wife or mom anymore; I was a worthy contributor to the conversation. And the other executives and "plus ones" were no longer intimidating to me, but fascinating individuals (and couples) with unique stories I admired and even learned from. All in all, not only had I became an expert at working the room, I had found a way that being a "plus one" could enable me to became a part of the fabric of the company that my husband care so much about. And I'd honed a valuable skill. Learning how to network with complete strangers, staying vulnerable and authentic in my approach, and reading their story, style and brand is a big reason why I am here today.

History Must Not Repeat Itself

It was the fall of 2011, and it only took one look at my mom, as I went to hug her in the baggage claim area at Chicago's O'Hare International Airport, to see that her eyes were shifting. She was yellow, barely able to walk on her own and her answers were foggy. My dad stood nearby, hugging JJ and Evan and keeping them distracted. The emotions in the air were almost palpable. We loaded the car and headed home, having said very little.

As I merged onto Interstate 294 North, I glanced at my mom, who was seated next to me and had just reached down to pick up my keys from the cup holder. Trying to put the house key into the air conditioning ducts, she was quietly "going to let the butterflies come out to fly." Asking her to look at me, I saw that the glaze had taken over. Something was happening and it was happening fast. I made eye contact with my dad and gave him that familiar look. She was sick again and we needed to go quickly.

History had taught us that my mom could go from a simple infection to being septic and in a fight for her life, and it could happen quickly. What I didn't know was how much time we had before things might get really dire.

I quickly thought of my boys and glimpsed my dad in the rearview mirror doing with my sons what he had always done with my brother and me when we were growing up. He was making them laugh, tickling them and, most importantly, diverting their attention away from the front seat and the grandmother who was ill and the mother who was beginning to panic. Within a split second, I was suddenly hit by a flashback. I remembered the sounds of an ambulance, the bright lights and sirens, and the feeling of the unknown as the ER staff rushed to the car before Dad had put the car in park.

But I was still driving on the interstate, unsure what to do in this moment. *"My children should not have to live through what I did,"* I kept telling myself, as it played on repeat from within. JJ and Evan were the exact age that my brother and I were when my mom first got sick. I didn't want them to spend any of their childhoods in hospitals, if I could help it.

As I started to come up with a plan of attack, I realized that this time, my dad and I were flying solo. We didn't have the neighbors across the street or other family members nearby to handle the kids. Dave was on a business trip. I was clueless as to which hospital to go to, how far away it was, and whether the staff could handle my mom's condition. We didn't have her doctors on call at Stanford nor would we be able to have her records on hand when we showed up to hospital. We were alone ... or so I felt.

I called my friend Lynn to find out where the closest hospital was and asked her to meet me at the house. As soon as we dropped off the boys with Lynn, we rushed to the ER. It took 26 minutes to drive from the airport to my home and another seven minutes to arrive at Northwestern Hospital in Evanston. By the time we got my mom to the ER, with nurses and doctors meeting us at the curb, my mom was too weak to sit up and slid right into the wheelchair.

With Dave on a flight home and my dad staying the night at the hospital, I headed back to the house to put the kids to bed. I was so grateful to have Lynn there for me and will never forget walking into my bedroom to find her lying down, with Evan curled up next to her fast asleep. I had built an incredible support system, yet, I still felt alone. That night had brought me back to the uncertainty and fear of my childhood.

It turned out that over the course of the four-hour plane flight from San Francisco to Chicago, my mom's simple cold had led to sepsis. She would spend the next week in the hospital and another week on my couch before her lungs were healed enough for the flight home.

Life continued and Dave and I began to think about staying in the Chicago suburbs for the long term to raise the boys. We bought a house and started renovations. However, construction ran overtime and over budget. We lived in a hotel for weeks at a time and when we thought we could handle it, we moved back into the house, spending most of our days crowded in our master bedroom. While Dave traveled, I managed the boys' schedules and activities, as well as the renovation punch list that never seemed to end. Just as construction was close to completion, we were hit with a storm that flooded our basement with four feet of sewage water. Our wedding and childhood photos were destroyed, as well as our furniture.

Then, in the spring of 2012, my mom visited again and, like the last time, fell ill and needed to be rushed to Northwestern. It was just too much for me to handle and I broke.

CHAPTER 3

Losing My Voice to Find Myself

Within 22 months of leaving the San Francisco Bay Area, we had lived in three homes, sold two of them, almost lost my mother twice, and had resided in two states. I had lost 15 pounds and was beginning to disconnect from my closest friends — struggling to find true joy in my everyday life. I fought hard to be present as a mom when, inside, I was numb.

What I remember next comes in bits and pieces.

Mom and Dad were visiting again, and Mom was sick. Seeing her like this — as I had so many times — broke me. Memories had come flooding back into my mind and I was hit hard by the fear that my children were about to experience what I had experienced so many times before. My heart was shattering. I couldn't breathe. Desperation, fear, anger and sadness descended.

Dave was in the city, hosting an executive from San Francisco for the official launch of the Chicago office. The timing couldn't have been worse. He was celebrating an incredible achievement and here I was, 25 miles away, falling apart.

"I can't do this anymore," I told Dave. "I need you to come home."

And he did.

Dave found me rocking in the corner of the shower, the hot water streaming down on my back as I silently cried and repeated to myself, "I can't do this anymore. It's not fair. They can't see this. My childhood will not be theirs."

He opened the door to the shower. Fully dressed, and without hesitation, he stepped in, picked me up, turned off the water and carried me to bed. Curled up in a ball, I asked for my mom. He helped her up the stairs so that she could lie with me. He then took JJ and Evan to Lynn's house for the night.

I was completely exhausted and burned out. My anxiety was at an all-time high, insomnia was a constant and I didn't know how to get out of my suffocating cycle. But what I *did* know was that my healing needed to start back home ... in California.

And so we went. It felt good to be back and to see my boys reconnect with the life they had left. I continued to work with my therapist back in Chicago and I even felt that my anxiety was under control. My weight was slowly stabilizing, and I began to reach out to close friends. So, when Dave told me he had signed me up to attend a Tony Robbins empowerment course in New Jersey, I can honestly say that I was surprised.

Lying Flat on a Cold Cement Floor

Since I was young, my parents had always instilled the belief that I could overcome anything. In fact, my dad was one of the early attendees of this acclaimed empowerment course when I was in high school. He came back with such a renewed sense of himself and outlook on life. My husband had been rejuvenated at the course as well, but when I asked why, both kept telling me it was hard to explain and understand unless you experience it firsthand. So, I left for New Jersey, open and ready for my own experience.

It was hard to leave the boys behind, but Dave encouraged me to take this time to figure out what made me happy. "Be vulnerable and do what you need to do," he told me. "I've got the boys and don't call home. We will be here when you get back."

Attending a course like this had never been a dream of mine nor did I think I needed to go. While it seemed like an event that could be interesting and moving, I didn't expect it to be life-changing. I imagined an extremely tall man on stage, yelling at his audience to motivate them, glimpses of people walking on hot coals and thousands of people jumping around in a huge convention hall.

When I arrived at the conference and was waiting to check in, most people around me talked about how nervous they were to walk on fire.

"Funny," I thought. *"That part doesn't seem like a big deal."* What I was thinking about was much more terrifying.

"What if I let everything out?" I considered. *"... all my regrets, fears, guilt, wishes, hopes and sadness that have been balled up inside me since I tagged out of the workforce, or even more unnerving, what if I share those stories of growing up that I have learned to keep inside?"*

Within the first hour, we were standing up, jumping around, singing, introducing ourselves to each other, sharing stories, hearing struggles, and identifying the truth about what and who we believed we were. By mid-afternoon that day, my first assignment was to write down my "story" so that I could share it with others, and I was confident I was ahead of the game. As a 36-year-old mother who had a mom with lupus, I figured I had a deep understanding of putting life into perspective. It should have been nothing for me to write down who I was, what I believed in and to share it with my fellow attendees. I was wrong. It was exhausting, but I was hooked.

Diving deep into myself hit me hard. What I feared more than walking on fire was being pushed to be honest, to be raw and to verbalize who I was, where I was in life and, most importantly, what I truly wanted to do with my life. That evening I wasn't sure what I wanted ... but I did realize that I needed to find *me*.

By the second day, I was losing my voice from yelling out "I am POWERFUL!" or screaming a hope or dream into the air. The more we verbalized our intents, the more my internal floodgates opened, and I couldn't scream the words loud enough. I wanted to scream *louder*.

As crazy as it sounds, the bonds I created in my group of five incredible people during those 72 hours were intense and special. It was that group who were the first to recognize who I was, and they encouraged me to believe that I could do anything I possibly wanted to. They reminded me that I had so much value to add to the world.

In fact, I will be forever grateful to the group who told me that I was "a force to be reckoned with," that my drive to fight for myself and desire to help others to do the same couldn't be tamed. And I will never forget that feeling of pure shock when I knew, deep down, that they were right. Actually, I had known it all along but now others recognized it too. I felt *seen*.

At the end of the day, each attendee was asked to find a spot on the floor to lie down. We closed our eyes and listened to a booming voice taking us through a visualization journey. First, we were invited to look back on our lives, and then we were encouraged to project 10 years into the future. On the convention center cement floor, with our eyes closed for almost three hours, we were led through the most powerful intellectual and emotional exercises I have ever attempted.

We started by recalling our earliest childhood memory. I went back to age three, where I was sitting next to that oak table in the kitchen, where my mom laid her wedding rings and enveloped me with a deep love as she crumbled on the inside. From that memory, we pulled out more recent ones and I found myself reflecting on experiences from my childhood through my teen years. I spent some time reflecting on my college life, as well as memories from when I was working full-time and through my transition to raising kids. Throughout the exercise, I reviewed my life as a mother, wife, daughter, sister and friend. As I relived my life in my mind, I realized that many of my childhood stories (stories I would use to explain who I was) involved lupus. And where lupus was connected to me meant that they were also shared stories about my mom. In fact, I was just as much a part of her story as she was a part of mine.

This distinction was huge, and when I reflected on it more, I finally realized that lupus is my *mom's* story, not mine. Sure, lupus had a huge influence on my childhood, my thought process, my ability to read a room, and my perspective in life, but her chronic illness doesn't define *me*.

So, I decided it was time that I removed lupus from my personal story that afternoon. Almost immediately, an incredible sense of clarity came over me. I remembered, for the first time in years, how much I loved to dance. I could feel how free my soul was when I was on stage and when I had dance parties with my children. I realized that I was a gifted athlete, that helping other people refueled me, that I thrived and survived in a crisis, and that I was most energized when I could make a change in other people's lives. I continued to unveil more defining stories as I completed the course's exercises. And as I accepted each, I began to redefine Janel in the present.

I asked myself, *"How do you stop participating in the story that is not yours?"* The answer was by reviewing each of the experiences in my mind once more and then letting them go. I honored my childhood memories of lupus, but I didn't have to save them with the memories I wanted to keep. To move forward in my life, I needed to release the past that no longer served me.

The next part of the exercise was even more profound. Still lying on the floor, my eyes wet from tears of joy, pain and lost memories, I was challenged to think ahead to the future. The booming but soothing voice asked, "If there were no limiting beliefs in your mind — no set stories from your past that held you back and only the knowledge you have the ability to achieve your dreams — then what would that look like? What would that feel like? Who would be around you? Where would you be? What would you be doing tomorrow ... next year ... or 10 years from now?"

I didn't know what I wanted to do, but I did know that I wanted to run my own company. I wanted to help other women find themselves and redefine their stories. I wanted to give women the permission to let go so they could believe big and view fear as fuel for achieving their dreams.

I wanted to give women the permission to let go so they could believe big and view fear as fuel for achieving their dreams.

The weekend continued. I yelled. I danced. I walked on fire. I completely lost my voice. But none of that mattered, because I had found me. And I was grateful. Grateful for my husband — the man who had believed in me when I no longer did. Dave had been by my side, unwavering during those tough years in Chicago. He had picked me up when I couldn't stand on my own, and on that day, I realized that by sending me to this course, Dave had given me the chance to stand on my own.

Coming home was an honest and genuine act of choosing my life, my husband, my boys and the family we had created. I vividly remember peeking out the window of the taxi when I pulled up to the house and saw the boys waving and holding up "welcome home" signs made just for me.

After filling the boys up with hugs and kisses, they ran back inside. It was then that I noticed a strange look on my husband's face. I couldn't put my finger on just what was different until I noticed a tear glistening in the corner of his eye. Dave doesn't often cry, so I knew this was a moment of importance. When I asked him what was wrong, he met my eyes and quietly said, "I didn't know if you'd come back."

Section 2

THE STYLE OF A STARTUP

"Passion is the backup generator when all else fails."

\- Carmine Gallo

Behind the Scenes: Face the Cold

It was 10 degrees outside with a wind-chill in the single digits when I walked into Lincoln Center. Standing in the middle of the square, wearing a borrowed $5,000 designer jacket whose name I couldn't even pronounce, I looked around and questioned what I was doing there. It was New York Fashion Week, February of 2015.

My face was frozen. I couldn't feel my fingers and had lost sensation in my toes two hours ago. I knew nobody in the industry. I had not a single ticket to a single runway show. I had no idea where the events were even being held. If Dolce & Gabbana walked by, I wouldn't have been able to even tell who was who. Truth be told, I didn't even know that they were two people.

I was lost on one of the biggest stages in the fashion world, but I knew what I needed to do ... it was time to give the performance of a lifetime. I was the choreographer, the storyteller and the dancer. I had the opportunity to create my own story ... a new story, yet again. But to do so, I had to change the conversation inside my mind. I remember telling myself, *"Pretend like you have been here before. Walk like you own the place and believe that you belong in this industry. What you do, who you are and why you are here matters."*

I took a deep breath, told myself that I had nothing to lose and went for it. With my first three steps around Lincoln Center's famous fountain, I began to feel powerful, bold and confident. I walked for hours, commanding attention from anyone I made eye contact with. Being here mattered.

I was determined to get photographed and posted on social media. Honestly, getting photographed in that outfit was *the* main reason why I flew out to New York. I wanted to play the game — to be part of the conversation and the hype in the fashion industry — and I knew that social media was my launch pad.

I spoke to as many people as I possibly could, asking them to take a picture with me and slowly I began to build a network of stylists, bloggers, photographers, writers and influencers. I learned why they loved fashion, why they were attending the event, who their favorite designers were and what they hoped to do in their careers. In fact, I met my first intern at that fountain. We talked about photography and the beauty of fashion as an art form.

Then, finally, it happened. I was asked if I would be in a quick photo shoot. My jacket had been noticed. And so had I.

Standing on the top stairs at the Lincoln Center, the FACE THE COLD photograph (as it was later captioned) was taken by an incredible photographer, Armandoz. The image was stunning. I'll never forget when I saw his post on Instagram. It was a game changer for me, as it not only created a huge shift in how I saw myself, but it instantaneously validated me and my mission. For with that single image, I became Janel Dyan.

CHAPTER 4

Simple. Beautiful. Chaos.

Let's be clear. It wasn't like I walked out of the empowerment course, flew home and decided to start a company centered around style and fashion. From 2007 to 2014, I wandered in so many directions that took me down so many different paths as I dipped my toes into the work world, trying to find a purpose beyond being a stay-at-home mom.

Back to the Bar

In 2007, I started working again by teaching at The Bar Method. Founded by Burr Leonard, the method was created after she discovered the Lotte Berk Method. Inspired to create her own version of a ballet barre workout, she developed "exercise techniques that would empower women of all ages and physical abilities ... to build healthy bodies for life."[1] To be fair, I was still struggling to shed the last 20 pounds of baby weight from my second pregnancy and the local studio had a deal for new students: unlimited classes for the first month. They promised that, if I took classes three days a week, my body would be transformed, inches would be lost and muscles would be built. Not believing it was true, I took the challenge and ended up going 28 days that month. They were right. But more importantly,

---

1 www.BarMethod.com/our-story/

what I wasn't prepared for was the immediate feeling that I was back in ballet class. The music, choreography and technique all came flooding back to me.

I was hooked. I signed up for the training classes so I could become a Bar Method instructor. Not only was I able work with women to empower them in building physical strength and healthier bodies, but I had, for the first time in a long time, found a home where I was someone beyond a mother or wife. I was merely "Janel." It felt like I had rediscovered a world that was my own. The women I taught and the instructors who I eventually mentored were phenomenal, yet the reality was it wasn't a career for me. It was an incredible outlet to get back into shape and a great bridge to get me through the early years, but it wasn't my true calling or a career I could envision moving forward with. It was a steppingstone.

Trunk Shows and Shutters

One year for Christmas, with a house full of family visiting from New York and limited bedrooms to offer, our living room became an impromptu bedroom. With a queen bed and a couch in the middle of the room, I realized that the large set of windows that faced out to the street needed to be covered. I knew that we needed plantation shutters for the room to help with their stay and general privacy moving forward, but we were on a tight budget and my husband didn't see the value of the investment. To be honest, he seemed to think that hanging up a few bed sheets would work fine and proceeded to cover the windows with white king-sized sheets! I just couldn't do it.

So, I decided that if I wanted shutters, and the extra money wasn't there, then I would make my own money and buy them myself. I reached out to a friend who had just hosted a Stella & Dot trunk show at my home and decided to give it a try as a stylist. It felt good to be able to bring in an income for the family and to feel like I had the ability to establish some financial independence, even if it was just to cover four windows. It was a powerful experience for me, and it didn't matter that it wasn't my dream job. I did enjoy my time at the trunk shows. I loved spending an evening helping women learn how to wear pieces for their lifestyles, updating their looks and, most importantly, I reveled in building a story with each piece they put on. What I quickly learned, however, was that I hate selling products. After two months, I had earned enough to have the shutters installed and I quit.

I didn't work again until after I returned from Chicago and had found myself by losing my voice in New Jersey.

My Stories, My Style, My Closet

I had walked on fire, had yelled all my fears to the point of losing my voice, had embraced my most intimate dreams and had come home with a renewed sense of self. However, the biggest shift happened the morning after I returned home. When I opened my closet, what I saw no longer reflected how I felt inside. Not a single piece of clothing made sense for the person I had become nor the woman I wanted to be.

On the left side of my closet hung clothes that no longer fit but that I couldn't let go of. They all had stories to tell ... pieces that I held onto thinking that *"someday I'll get back into that size."* There were dresses that I only wore during the holidays, Banana Republic pants from my first job out of school, shirts that I couldn't even button over my chest, and jeans that I loved so much during college but couldn't pull up over my thighs. These were the outfits and the stories that reminded me of my life before kids.

On the right side of the closet were the clothes that I wore at my heaviest. These were the clothes that I hadn't spent too much money on because I was ashamed of what my body had become (sizes that were four sizes up from the ones on the left.) They were my *"just in case I get bigger or pregnant again"* pieces. They were also the clothes that I reached for when I wanted to cover up my stomach or hide my arms because I felt fat or out of shape or embarrassed of the muffin top that hung over my jeans.

I had spent three days learning to let go of my past stories so that I could make room for new ones and, yet, my closet didn't reflect my mental shift. In fact, I felt immediately thrown back into a rut. These pieces were a reminder of the career I walked away from and a body that was no longer mine. So, for me to move forward, they had to go.

I needed to leave my "old-body stories" behind and shift to a new one, a story of strength and the sacrifice you give as a mother. It could become an equalizer with other mothers, a conversation starter with new moms and a badge of honor.

I remember asking myself, *"What is my story? What stories do I want to share? What conversation do I want my outfits to start?"*

I still had the extra skin, the stretch marks and the cellulite — but I was no longer ashamed of them. These clothes represented the postpartum depression, the struggle for my identity, motherhood and the journey I went through. Instead of dressing to hide my body, I decided to embrace it. So I built a new wardrobe that felt right. Every morning afterward, I opened the closet and loved what I saw. I had confidence in myself, I carried myself differently and I became more engaged with my children, my marriage and my friendships. People noticed ... and so did I.

Soon after, I packed up my pre-pregnancy weight clothes and found another mom to share them with ... a mom who could use a boost of confidence and the clothes to feel it.

As I had done years before with my Banana Republic and J. Crew looks, I was ready to reinvest in my personal brand. I let go of asking myself what I was going to wear today and started asking myself what my story was today. By aligning who I was on the inside to what I wore on the outside, I felt proud of myself, empowered by my stories and excited to get dressed each morning.

I let go of asking myself what I was going to wear today and started asking myself what my story was today.

My style shifted immediately. I no longer put on workout pants and a comfortable sweatshirt. Instead, I bought jeans that fit my current size, found fun flats that could add pops of color to each outfit and established a look that hinged on what continues to be my signature piece — a simple white T-shirt. If I ever found myself struggling with the clothing size number, I simply cut out the tag, refusing to let a size determine how I felt about myself. It didn't matter. I did.

Without knowing it, I was establishing the foundation of what would drive my business today — building a brand that starts with a story, grows with the style, controls the conversation and ends with an authentic and relatable new brand.

Without knowing it, I was establishing the foundation of what would drive my business today – building a brand that starts with a story, grows with the style, controls the conversation and ends with an authentic and relatable new brand.

Toes in the Grass

A few weeks after I settled in back home, someone I had met at the empowerment course reached out to see how I was holding up and to ask for some business advice. He ended up hiring me to consult with his seed-and-turf company. They needed help creating an event-marketing plan for a trade show and he thought an outside view would be valuable. This was the first time in a long time that someone saw potential in me, wanted to work with me and was willing to pay for my creativity even though I had no experience. I dove right in. I had to relearn Microsoft PowerPoint and Excel. I brushed up on event management and jumped into product marketing. It was slow-going at first. What takes me an hour to complete today took me almost a day of work back then. It wasn't much, but it was a paycheck and a place start.

Curbside Counseling

Many mornings, after dropping off Evan at preschool, I stood on that same curb outside the front gate to catch up with other moms. We were usually in no rush because pick-up was only two hours away. We would talk about everything from boob sweat, sleepless nights, marriage, dreams of going back to work or wanting to tag out, finding outlets that could be our own, child development courses, books to read, volunteering woes, shopping, nutrition and body issues. Our lives had many common threads that, at the heart of it all, started with simply sharing our stories, seeing ourselves as beautiful and embracing the chaos of motherhood.

The countless chats that took place on the curb helped me realize that my strengths today were the same strengths I had as a little girl so long ago. I was using my intuition — my ability to read each of them — with every conversation and tailoring my advice around the woman I was talking to. Soon, we nicknamed these talks "curbside counseling."

The conversations would often end up on the topic of style, finding clothes that fit and feeling guilty spending money on ourselves. I enjoyed sharing my tips and amazing finds at retail stores and, over time, my group of friends started to lean on me for what to wear. It didn't feel like I was doing anything unique, but I had become the go-to friend for style advice.

I had become the go-to friend for style advice.

What I offered was more than insights on child tantrums and body image acceptance. Instead, I gave each of the women permission to be vulnerable and authentic.

Without thinking about it, I simply read each woman. Just as I had done as a child, I listened to the stories she shared, watched her body language and the clothes she chose to wear, and followed what she decided to share in a group conversation. That ability that I honed as a young girl — the ability to quickly find a common ground and alignment of our stories — would manifest into identifying a piece of my outfit that she related to and could "pull off" herself. I had unconsciously mastered the ability to establish trust by simply aligning my story and style to the journey that she was on.

Crossing the Threshold

On that very curb, I met a mother (and an incredible entrepreneur) who ended up being the catalyst I needed to jump back into the corporate world. We got to know each other during impromptu school playdates in the afternoons. As we watched our kids run around, our conversations always seemed to find their way to the industry she worked in, the work she was doing and the need for establishing a solid foundation to grow the company. I started to look forward to seeing her at drop-off or pick-up for her kids so I could hear about her progress, celebrate her wins and, when needed, give her advice on ways to get through a challenge.

I went home and pulled out reports I had written years ago and performance management implementation handbooks that I had crafted. Listening to her, I became inspired to read as much as I could about the newest methods of running a small company.

"Could I hire you?!" she asked me one day. I couldn't say no and, to be honest, I didn't want to. She and her business partner ran a women-owned social impact consulting firm that provided strategy and communications services to nonprofits, public agencies and philanthropic organizations.

I quickly established my new business, Threshold Consulting, to not only get paid but to restart my corporate career. I chose the name as a symbol of taking that first step to cross over the threshold from a start-up with a great idea to an established company. It was just me, my outdated HR certifications and the grit to start again.

Like any start-up that was about to hit a rapid growth phase, I felt confident that I could be a value-add with their hiring, employee onboarding and enablement, and strategic operational processes. But they needed help in other places too. They were outgrowing their office and needed advice about ways to scale their physical space. We also explored the implementation of a CRM (Client Relations Management) solution to track contacts, projects and opportunities. Anything I didn't know I'd quietly and quickly learn.

I remember one day sitting across the table from them, listening to how they launched the company four years prior, and thinking that this should be me. It was then that I realized running Threshold wasn't what I wanted. It was then that I realized I wasn't that 27-year-old who had thrived and loved working in the corporate world. Everything that I thought it would be was no longer what I wanted. I wanted something more ... something that was completely and entirely my own ... something that was driven by passion and made me want to get up every single day.

What I *did* know was that I didn't want to be a Bar Method teacher. I wasn't interested in selling jewelry. I didn't want to build marketing plans for companies that weren't my own. I didn't want to be a business consultant. I had already done all that, and I no longer wanted to be a stay-at-home mom.

As I had learned months earlier during the empowerment course, I knew I needed to write it all down: my hopes, my goals, my dream job and the answer to, what I believe, is the most powerful question of all: *"What would I do if 'no' was never the answer?"*

So, I went back to my notebook and at the very top of page one, I wrote: "I want to give women the permission I never gave myself." What's funny is that, by writing it down, I had just given myself permission to take that first step and commit to it being *my* turn to say yes to *my* dreams.

I want to give women the permission I never gave myself.

I wanted to help women accept their own bodies. I wanted to help women style themselves to reflect who they truly are. I wanted to build a company that was an influential force to empower women to find the permission to take each step with confidence, vulnerability and authenticity.

Making the KUT

In the summer of 2014, I answered a call that would set the course. It was a fork that led down a path that would launch me into a world that I never imagined myself being a part of — the fashion industry.

As the boys were jumping on the trampoline with my husband one late afternoon, Catherine, a friend and mom, called to ask if I had some time to meet with her sister-in-law who was in town from Los Angeles. Known as "the voice" of the brand, Lauren, was launching a pilot project to create a brand identity for a fashion retail company called KUT from the Kloth. Working closely with the lead designer, she was looking to recruit five "strong women" from all over the country to participate in a "Style Muse" program. She was seeking women who had a unique sense of style and, that day, was looking for an ambassador within the Bay Area.

Lauren showed up at my house, carrying two huge boxes filled with jeans, which are items in my closet that make up a large part of my wardrobe. I was immediately excited to try things on. Like most women, once I find a denim brand that works for me, I don't buy anything else. I was an Adriano Goldschmied "AG" girl. But I did love jeans and was always open to test things out and give my honest feedback. To be fair, I had never heard of KUT, but after I tried on my first pair of "Mia Skinny Jeans," I was hooked. Even better, the price point was one where most of the moms I knew wouldn't feel guilty buying them.

We spent the next few hours drinking wine, building looks from my wardrobe and having an impromptu photoshoot. With my remaining Stella & Dot jewelry spread out in their display cases, half of my current closet laying throughout the living room and several styles of jeans inside-out on the couch — I had inadvertently become a stylist. With each outfit, I began to establish a story that would go along with the look, and every time I changed accessories, I would change the story.

Lauren's personality was infectious. Full of life, expressive and grateful — she validated everything I was doing. She was fascinated by the way I would build an outfit based on a narrative, not just on what the trend was, and made me feel empowered by my unique process. We took turns taking pictures in my backyard, on the deck, at the front doorway and in the front yard. We were three women laughing and playing dress up.

By that evening, I agreed to join the "Style Muse" program. On September 2, 2014, I was officially introduced as a style muse for KUT from the Kloth, giving me my first glimpse into the fashion industry. So, I took this great opportunity to leverage their brand in order to amplify mine.

Then reality hit when Lauren told me that my first blog, a mini article, and lifestyle pictures were due a few days after. I didn't know where to start. I had no professional profile of my own on social media. I had never posted a blog. I didn't have a Twitter account or an updated LinkedIn profile. My personal Instagram looked mediocre at best. I had no idea how to leverage the influencer market and what a social media strategy plan was all about. I hadn't mastered the art of taking a selfie, had never asked others to help take full-body photos and struggled with the right approach to blogging about the KUT pieces.

I also needed a landing page (some would say a validation page) to share who I was, my back story and why I had decided to enter the world of fashion as a style muse and a blogger.

Three Nights, One Couch

No joke ... I spent so much time on that couch that I left a permanent divot!

I established my new company in three nights. I worked each night after the boys went to bed, into the wee hours of the morning, writing content, creating inspiration boards, reading articles and making endless checklists on how to get started. My husband found me asleep with notebooks spread everywhere in the morning with one son laying sideways on me and a computer that had lost all its battery hours before. (Let's be fair, this still happens, just on a bigger couch now that the boys are older and taller!)

I built my first Blogspot site as *Simple. Beautiful. Chaos.* It was my own site and my own voice. It represented my perspective of simply being grateful for the life you have, feeling beautiful as you are and honoring the craziness and chaos of motherhood.

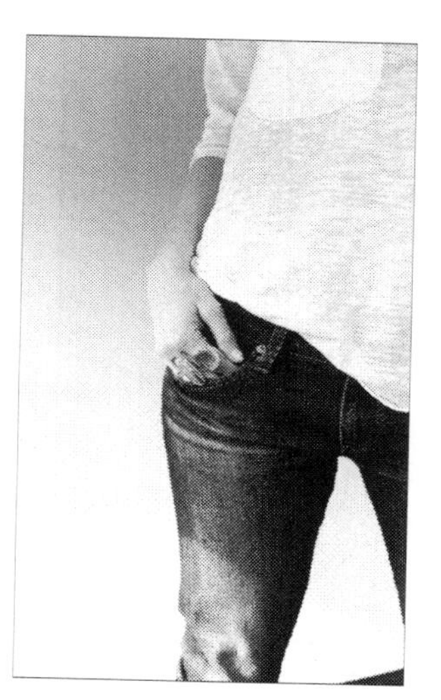

Then, I tried to write my first article. It was supposed to be a simple 150-word blog post. It was hard. I'm not sure how you get writer's block on a straightforward article, but it took me two nights to finish "A Simple White T-shirt." I started over so many times that I lost count. I was paralyzed to finish because I feared that the article wouldn't make sense, or the editor would consider it pointless. I was worried that my advice on how I styled a white T-shirt, with the now known "JD two-finger tuck" would be seen as totally useless. I was terrified to post my first social media post on Instagram, as I was extremely vulnerable to criticism and rejection. Although my company wasn't much of a business yet, I posted it anyway and it felt incredible.

Nineteen days later, I posted my second blog post and, with that, included the company's first tagline and vision that I hoped to share with others. These three statements are the foundation of JD's First Three Steps.

> **Reclaim** my sense of style. **Redefine** the chaos in my life. **Rediscover** me.

A new journey had just begun.

CHAPTER 5
Starting the Conversation

It's 8:00 a.m., I'm two cups of coffee deep and the butterflies are fluttering. I'm excited. Today is my client's first step to finding confidence in herself and her wardrobe. It is the beginning of a new chapter – one that she will write with authenticity and vulnerability.

Standing outside of her front door with my assistant, my tailor and two rolling racks, I ring the doorbell. In moments like this, I always find myself with my stomach in knots, eager to know more about my client and a tad nervous for the journey we are about to embark on together.

I know that she is about to go through an intensive experience that will leave her (and me) physically and emotionally drained. Over the course of next four to five hours, I will ask her to try on every single item in her closet (everything, except her undergarments). It will be an experience that will challenge her to dig deep inside herself. But, if I do my job right, she will feel incredible and have newfound confidence in who she is and what she wears. She will no longer ask herself, "What am I going to wear today?" Instead, she will learn to ask, "What is my story?"

The door opens with her saying, "Okay, don't judge me. My closet is a mess and I know you are going to find so many things that are too old, outdated or no longer on trend. I'm sure you will tell me to get rid of everything."

"That's not going to happen," I smile reassuringly as we head back to her closet.

And so it begins.

JD Styled

Walking into a woman's closet requires a deep respect for a simple truth: this is one of the most vulnerable places for her to share with me. It is filled with memories of each phase of her life.

Walking into a woman's closet requires a deep respect for a simple truth: this is one of the most vulnerable places for her to share with me. It is filled with memories of each phase of her life.

There is the dress that was worn at her rehearsal dinner, and here is her grandmother's overcoat, which she used to try on and fall asleep in. She has the jumpsuit that she bought on a whim (because she was invited to an event and had nothing to wear) and there is the blazer that she wore for the biggest interview of her career. She shows me the scarf that her daughter had given her for Mother's Day and the most expensive outfit that she's ever splurged on, with tags, that she's never worn. She shares that she feels guilty for wasting the money but that she bought it "on sale," so it's not so bad. There are tags on jeans and tops because she isn't sure she will wear them or doesn't know how to wear them. There are shoes that she hasn't worn in years and some left in boxes ... but can't part with any of them because they are so beautiful. I'll find a handbag she splurged on because her friends told her that it was worth it, but still hasn't had the right "occasion" to pull it out. And then there's the item that she has to keep, but will never use, because it was a gift from someone she loves.

I ask her to walk me through how she gets dressed in the morning — how she builds an outfit and what pieces she starts with — which gives me insight into her thought process. I look at how many pieces she has. There are loads of tops, jeans, overcoats, shoes and accessories. I ask her why she starts with a specific item and then request that she builds a few of her favorite looks.

Most women start with the areas of their body with which they have the *most* confidence or the least. Shoes, overcoats, accessories and handbags are usually the confidence builders when they aren't happy with their body weight. Jeans and tops are usually the areas that trigger the most insecurity. Typically, it's one or the other — hips and thighs or arms and stomach.

As my team empties the closet, I watch what pieces she gravitates toward on the racks and listen to the stories she shares about them. She discovers pieces that she has forgotten, ones that she will "never part with" and the reasons why she bought items that she now regrets. The simple act of touching each article of clothing brings an emotion and visceral reaction. *This* is what I am here for. I am not here to judge her decisions or the stories she shares. It's quite the opposite. I am here to learn about her through her stories, her buying habits and the clothes she has chosen. My goal is to make sure that her stories and style align authentically.

In the bedroom or the closet, she stands in nothing but her undergarments. She may move to cover herself initially, but that reflex lessens as the hours pass. Our trust builds and her stories are "lived in" once more with each piece she tries on. By starting this way, she becomes physically vulnerable and ready to be emotionally courageous as well.

I stand behind her as she looks at her reflection. Dressed in all black, I fade into the background for this experience is not about me. It's about her seeing her true self in the mirror. I don't want to be noticed and, for now, my opinion doesn't matter as much as hers. She covers up her thighs, sucks in her stomach, grabs her upper arms and makes comments about everything she could improve. It's hard, at times, to hear these comments because I've said them to myself. And, more importantly, I don't see what she is looking at. We are truly our own worst critics.

All clients are different, and each reacts to this part of the experience uniquely. But I never take for granted each client's reaction to being physically and emotionally naked and vulnerable, for I see it as an honor that I get to be standing in the room with them. I also know it means that she is ready ... ready to let go of stories, to keep stories and to make room for new stories.

She is ready ... ready to let go of stories, to keep stories and to make room for new stories.

This experience is a marathon and the entire JD team wants to see her to the finish line. I navigate through her clothes, rack after rack. My team takes clothes off the hangers, folds them in piles and hangs them back up. My tailor is a few steps away to review any piece that needs fixing or reconstructing. The process is seamless, and the clothes she keeps are returned and organized back into her closet. When I work with my client, I am focused entirely on her while my team is focused on making sure the momentum continues.

The Stories Are What Matters Most

"OK, so let's start with walking me through your typical day. What is your go-to outfit?" With a slight hesitation, she begins to build her look. How she does this is what I am most interested in. What area of her closet does she gravitate to? Which piece does she start with and where does she get stuck in the process? Walking back out to show me the look, I simply say, "Tell me the story behind this look."

It's both a question and an invitation, and one that she may not have expected to hear from me. My goal is to disrupt her preconceived idea of what my role will be; I'm not here to dress her up ... I'm here to help her rediscover who she is. It is so important that I gain her trust and give her the control to lead the day, to feel safe to share and believe that I am unconditionally present for her.

I want her to find her voice. I want to hear how she narrates her stories and why she chooses each piece to amplify them. There is no right or wrong choice that she has made. Each piece was purchased for a reason and so I honor it.

I want her to find her voice. I want to hear how she narrates her stories and why she chooses each piece to amplify them.

There also is no one way to do what I do. Every appointment is unique to each client. There is no set outline of questions that have been written down. The questions I ask are directed by the answers she gives and the life she lives. It is a collaboration.

"Ok, why did you buy this jacket?"

"Did you buy this outfit all at once?"

> *"What do you love about it?"*
>
> *"What doesn't work for you?"*
>
> *"Where have your worn it?"*
>
> *"How does it make you feel?"*

I read her body language. I read the way she tugs at her blouse, trying to cover her stomach, and the way she pulls down on her jeans to try to feel more comfortable with her thighs. I read the way she reaches for shoes to give her height in her A-line dress so that she feels taller and leaner. She looks for a sweater to cover her backside and explains to me that the current dress "used to fit" but she's holding onto it for when she loses a little weight.

I am less concerned, at that point, about the style but more about how it makes her feel and what her body does when she stands in front of the mirror. Our conversation is one of guidance, tutoring and validation. With each piece, each look, she learns about different necklines, what hemline works best for her, where to tailor her cropped pants to avoid "no man's land" and how to do the "two-finger tuck" with a top.

So, what does it look like when we've found a story and a style that aligns? It happens instantly and without her even realizing. Her shoulders go back. There is a slight lift in her chin. She may pucker her lips a bit and stand a bit taller while turning around a few times.

Nailed it. *That's* a story I want to know, the story I want her keep and the style that is authentically hers. (I'm not going to lie, and my clients will tell you, I always get chills when it happens.)

When she becomes more confident in her story and her ability to create a style of her own, she takes over the conversation. Putting on what used to be her favorite sweater and sharing the story behind it, it becomes clear whether she'll keeps it, hold to discuss later or let it go. She looks at that old favorite sweater and asks herself anew, "Is this my story today?"

Only she can answer that.

This entire process is full of emotion. It's a wave we ride together. When I can tell that she is fading, we break, hydrate, get a protein fix and power on. It is important that she sees the hanging clothes dwindle from the racks so that she remains focused and doesn't get too overwhelmed. She takes stock in watching my team begin to bring her favorite pieces back into her closet — establishing a wardrobe that she will love to wake up to. At the same time, the clothes that she no longer wants — the pieces that she has just lived one last time — are kept out of sight until we are done. The pile grows, as well, with purchases she now realizes aren't her style anymore and clothes that she has never worn. She's letting go and it feels good.

At the end of the appointment, my team brings in all the clothes she had decided to let go of. The bags of clothing now represent all her hard work today — the stories, the styles and the pieces that she no longer needs. For most of my clients, there is a physical sense of relief — as if weight has been lifted from her — as she celebrates all her hard work and her personal triumph. It's a cool experience to be a part of.

For the next two weeks, those bags go back to my office, and I ask her to live with just the pieces she has kept. We hold off on all new purchases and check in daily to support her new brand.

Over the years, I have learned that there are some clients who may have a few pieces that they want back. During those two weeks, if there are pieces that she suddenly looks for, then we add them back. If she can live without them for two weeks, then she doesn't need them.

Finally, with all the racks, bags, extra hangers and wardrobe rehung, she reenters her closet. Hanging up are the stories that are authentic to who she is today, that are relevant to the life she lives, and, above all, that give her joy every morning when she determines the story — the story she wants to share that day.

In the end, it isn't just about new looks, new purchases or an organized closet of clothes. It's about starting with the story, building her style to align with them and giving herself permission to be authentic in her brand.

The Birth of "Beyond Us"

There was a point after my work with KUT from the Kloth when I decided to do another overhaul in my closet because I noticed just how much clothing and how many accessories I had amassed over the previous year. It was too much. In fact, I remember walking over and immediately pulling out as much as I could. I felt gluttonous. By the end of that day, I had cleared out almost 50% of what I owned from every drawer and every closet in my house.

Bagging them up, I walked downstairs into my office to find all my extra accessories (like the remaining Stella & Dot jewelry that I no longer wore) and added them to the piles. With almost four large bags, I opened my storage closet and put them on top of more than six bags that two of my clients had let go of the week prior. With the bags staring back at me, I realized that there had to be women who

I knew — women within my community — who I could help style and pay it forward with these clothes. Instead of dropping these bags off at a donation center, I wanted to find women to give these pieces to, along with the stories these clothes had lived (just as I had done during those summers as a young girl). So, I decided to offer a private styling event to some of the most incredible teachers I knew. Women who, from the time I became a style muse, had supported and encouraged me to keep on going. These were teachers I would talk to while dropping off my boys at school.

I decided to host the event at my home one evening. I gathered up all my KUT jeans, hung up other tops and jackets, and laid out accessories. I did the same with the six large bags of my clients' clothing. What laid before me was pretty impressive.

Over a few bottles of wine, great music and lots of laughter, we talked about what they were wearing, the pieces that they had brought for style advice, trends of the market and the clothing I had laid out. The evening was about giving them the chance to try on looks to see if they liked different styles, cuts and colors. The best part came when I had the honor to share with them that most of these pieces they fell in love with that night had been gifted to them from the closets of my clients. Suddenly, the sense of community and shared experience expanded beyond that room.

Without knowing it then, I had just planted the seed for what would become a key value of JD and a part of what we do today. With the belief that stories need to be shared and clothes carry memories, I established "Beyond Us" in 2017, a platform of women empowering, supporting and investing in other women. I continue to strive to ensure that, in the eyes of our clients and our Beyond Us recipients, the pieces are not viewed as charity. They are simply clothes and accessories that have served to tell one woman's story and are now being repurposed to tell a new story for a different woman. Nothing is lost, but so much is gained.

The Story of Alaska

One afternoon, my dear friend Erin came into town to visit. We had a glass of wine and caught up in my office, which was full of clothes on racks, tagged to be donated for my client. There, she opened up about a friend of hers who was going through a rough time.

She was a young mom of three young children, and she lived in Alaska, 150 miles from the closest Target or other retail department store. Her youngest child was a few months old. Newly single and desperate to find a full-time job to cover her expenses, she had lost the confidence to go for an interview because she had nothing to wear. Her body didn't fit into her current wardrobe, and she couldn't afford to invest in a new one.

A few minutes later, I was on the phone talking to this incredible woman (who I will refer to as "Alaska"), learning more about what was going on. It was clear that she needed job security, but it was even more clear that she needed help for her interviews. Looking around my office, I knew the exact client who could help ... a client whose clothes were hanging on the racks in my office and who happened to be the same size as Alaska. There were some great styles for this very moment. I knew that "Alaska" would be my next Beyond Us girl.

With my client's permission, three days later, we gathered and sent more than $5,000 worth of clothing to Alaska. She had no idea, like the teachers, that this was headed her way. I wanted it to be a surprise. Included in the package was a simple note.

Alaska,

This is sent to you from a woman who wants you to know that you are not alone ... that there are women here in the Bay Area who believe in you. Enjoy these pieces of clothing, wear them and share them. In return, the only ask I have is if you could let me know how things are going and if these pieces have helped you find the confidence to take that next step you need and deserve.

xx – j

A week later, in a simple text message to Erin, Alaska asked Erin to let me know that she had never before had so much fun trying on clothes (that fit!) and had shared some pieces with other friends. She finally felt like she was back on her feet. (Months later, I learned that she found a job and life was getting better every day.)

When I share these stories, like Alaska's, to my clients, most of them respond with the same question — "What else can I give?" Yet, the question isn't so much about what clothing pieces they can give but rather what stories they could share to help create new ones.

A KUT Above

KUT from the Kloth gave me a platform to share my story through style and to launch my brand. This was an incredible opportunity to connect with women through honest conversations, vulnerable accounts of struggle and triumph, and a stylish look that was relatable to so many. As a style muse, I would choose three pieces from their newest line each month to wear and assess. I would post to my blog about why

I liked the pieces, how I would wear them and tips on how to style them. I would send in pictures to their marketing department for their social media blasts.

As I gained followers and success, KUT gave me more exposure to the business. They flew me down to Los Angeles to meet with their marketing team, spend time with Evelyn, the creative director, and learn from their manufacturing crew. I pretty much had a crash course on the behind-the-scenes of the fashion world.

I was absorbing as much as I could, loved the challenge and decided that if I wanted to accelerate faster, I needed a huge opportunity. So, I pitched them the idea to be their style muse on the ground during New York Fashion Week. It would be a great way to help KUT with their business goals and to amplify my brand at the same time.

KUT agreed, and for my second trip to New York Fashion Week in Fall 2015, I was sponsored. It wasn't a huge financial gain, but it gave me much more confidence as I was now the style muse of KUT and a representative of their new line. During that week, I gathered feedback about consumer demographics and how products are placed in retail stores, took pictures of my meetings and posted to social media from all over the events. But the truth was — I wasn't just there for KUT.

I wanted to make more connections and build the brand for the business, JD. I pushed myself to be completely open to learning about an elusive market that still didn't fully make sense to me. I was driven to understand the buying behavior of women. Why women bought what they did, when they bought most often during the year, why they would return or exchange their purchases, and what newest designers were trending. Every lead was important, even the ones that flopped, as they added experience to my new story and gave me context and confidence for the next one.

My success was dependent upon how large of a network I could cast. Building my client base, establishing relationships with brands and designers, and optimizing my social media platforms was my primary focus to growing JD. The hustle began in earnest during New York Fashion Week and continued when I returned home. Nothing about this was easy. I needed to establish myself as a company to work with and a style expert to be taken seriously, but I couldn't get my foot in the door unless I had thousands of followers on Instagram and worked with celebrities. Trying to play the game was complete distraction and very impersonal. I know it made complete sense from a business standpoint, but it felt like a diversion from what I was beginning to realize I wanted most: to give all women access into the world of fashion and permission for them to be a part of the conversation. Every woman is an influencer.

Every woman is an influencer.

To gain traction, I needed to better understand how the market worked and the buying behavior of women in fashion. I met with stylists to understand their business and walked into retail stores to learn about their brands, their customers and the buying habits of those customers. I reached out to anyone who understood how to build a social following to learn the tricks of the trade. I tried to maximize my social presence and make the most of my time by scheduling social posts and creating affiliations with brands that drove referral income.

No matter how hard I tried, my approach to building a following wasn't working for me ... not because it wasn't viable, but because it didn't feel authentic. I loathed the pressure to take selfies, the pressure to keep my weight down, and the intense pace of posts that were necessary to keep my following engaged. At times, I found myself paralyzed when it was time to write a post and constantly engrossed in Instagram and Twitter. It was apparent that I didn't want to grow the brand in this direction, but I couldn't figure out how to break into the fashion industry without it.

Limited Knowledge, Limitless Opportunities

Being an entrepreneur is a journey that can be lonely, insecure, uncomfortable, challenging and full of fear. Early on, not only did I lack experience, industry knowledge, fashion terminology (seriously, you should have heard how I used to pronounce "Givenchy") or a degree from fashion school, I had never had a passion for high fashion. My subscriptions were from *Time* and *Newsweek*, not *Cosmopolitan* or *Vogue*. There were times when it felt impossible and overwhelming to start a company when I didn't understand the market that I was working in. Saying I felt like an imposter is an understatement.

Being an entrepreneur is a journey that can be lonely, insecure, uncomfortable, challenging and full of fear.

"You either walk inside your story and own it or you stand outside your story and hustle for your worthiness."
– Brené Brown

My legitimacy couldn't be determined by a resume or experience. In order to build JD, I had to hustle, listen to feedback, tell my stories, learn and test the market, have failures and wins, and trust that my "why" was my biggest asset.

It impacted life at home. I had sleepless nights when I forgot to stock the fridge or make dinner for the kids. I had to rewash wet clothes left in the washer for days because they smelled of mildew.

I worked for weeks alone in my living room — day and night — with no one to bounce ideas off of. There was a sense of anxiety that lingered in the back of the mind, thinking:

> *"Am I doing enough?"*
>
> *"Do I really have the talent?"*
>
> *"Am I driving the business in the wrong direction and/or will it crash and burn no matter what I do?"*
>
> *"Can I deliver on what I promised my client or am I destined to come up short?"*

It's one thing to know what you don't know, but *not* knowing what you don't know is humbling, scary and vulnerable. But it is also an incredible opportunity to establish something without any preconceived ideas or known territory.

"Don't be intimidated by what you don't know. That can be your greatest strength and will ensure that you do things differently from everyone else."
- Sara Blakely

It can be a journey full of possibilities, a chance to think outside the box — or not have a box at all. I began to realize that my lack of experience could be one of my biggest assets. I was able to enter a space without any preconceived ideas and limitations. I could push the envelope without even knowing it and then develop what I couldn't find on the market — services and/or products. My approach to what I do is unique and difficult to copy.

Client First, Revenue Second

I made a decision that would prove, long-term, to be a huge asset and became one of my greatest differentiators. I changed my revenue structure. I wanted to be service-driven, not commission-focused. And in order to be as authentic and honest as possible with my clients and the sales associates I was working with, my company policy had to shift.

I wanted to be service-driven, not commission-focused.

I decided that no matter how much retail product my clients bought in a store or with a brand, JD would not make any commission from the purchases. Many people around me felt that this was company suicide. I had a small client base at the time and was barely generating revenue. But my gut was telling me otherwise.

No other stylists worked this way. It was the norm that stylists make their revenue on a combination of billable hours and a business-to-business commission based on what the client buys. Think about it. How many times do you question a sales associate's feedback or opinion when you know, at the end of the day, what they sell is tied to a commission? That mentality is the opposite of what JD stands for. Instead, my company was built on unwavering integrity, brutal honesty and always putting the client first. I never wanted even the illusion of split loyalties.

I have never been driven by making money first. It's always been about the clients, their narratives, their style and the services I provided to support them. My clients know that I have no biases on whether I put them in Target or Gucci because their clothing budgets are never tied to my income.

As I built relationships with a retail brand or sales associate, I made it clear that I wasn't looking to share commission, but rather looking to drive connections that helped both of us. In theory, my company could help clients make good decisions, provide honest feedback on client preferences of what works and what doesn't, pull pieces that have a high chance of staying in their closet and reduce the amount of returns — minimizing a salesperson's lost commissions. I had it figured out, but I knew that my success was now about establishing myself and JD's brand as a company to work with ... one that could bring in high net sales and consistent repeat clients.

I was building my brand as a style advisor for executive women in leadership, as well as a go-to expert for brands in New York that wanted to understand the Bay Area market.

My decision paid off. Doors opened, clients signed on and the company started seeing a return.

A Spade of Partnerships

In 2015, while working in New York, I walked through the enormous golden doors into the Kate Spade store on Madison Avenue. My goal was to establish a relationship allowing my New York clients VIP access to the store, as well as the ability to have pieces shipped out to the Bay Area when needed. Initiating the conversation was simple. Several of my clients were loyal shoppers there and were hoping to get a glimpse of their exclusive upcoming fall/winter line.

The Kate Spade team was incredible. Over the next two years, we collaborated on several private stylings in their private VIP room.

Each client had the opportunity to work with two dedicated stylists while lounging on a pink satin vintage sofa surrounded by bows and a table full of candy jars. Together, we sipped pink champagne and nibbled on sweet treats while she would try on her curated pieces.

In the beginning, knowing which clients to align with these events was difficult and involved financial risk for me. You see, each event at Kate Spade was expected to drive $3,000 of sales for the sales team, and if the client didn't spend that amount, it was important for me to invest in the difference to maintain my relationship with the store. I was hyper-aware that, in retail, it's all about commissions. There was a lot of risk from the start, but I had no other hand to play if I wanted to stay true to my company's values and build a reputation that JD is a brand you can work with.

The Keychain and the Dinosaur

While walking down Fifth Avenue, I walked by the window front of COACH. It's a brand that hadn't been on my radar or my clients' brand favorites list, but the store was filled with customers. It took a moment for me to see what was creating so much buzz, but then I saw the main attraction. Standing an impressive 13-feet tall and made up of more than 400 handbags was "Rexy the Dinosaur." The first floor was filled with futuristic, youthful and whimsical handbags and accessories featuring dinosaurs, spaceships and bold, bright colors. It was obvious that this wasn't the COACH I knew 20 years earlier. I decided to walk in.

And I didn't walk out empty handed. The company had recently launched a line of keychains and customizable leather baseball hats, a nod to their history of making wallets from the same hard, durable leather used in baseball mitts. The keychains and hats were emblazed with the logos of baseball teams, such as the Chicago Cubs and the San Francisco Giants. Given that my husband is a die-hard New York Yankee fan, and I had to leave with something, I bought the blue leather NY logoed keychain.

As it turns out, I met the most fascinating sales associate, Michael, while purchasing that item. Little did I imagine that a simple purchase would turn into an incredible relationship. His excitement about the products and deep loyalty to the brand was impressive. In a world full of apathy or insincere interest, Michael was the opposite. Not only was he ambitious in his own career, he was invested as an employee to the success of COACH. In turn, he was hungry to learn what was happening in the Bay Area, the different style trends that were happening on the west coast and the demographics of my client base.

That afternoon, I heard the entire story of COACH. I learned about the values of what the brand stands for, their commitment to their employees, their dedication to preserving the art of apprenticeship for the artisans who hand-crafted each leather goods (some of whom have been with the company for 30+ years), and the desire to invest in the ever-changing consumer market for technology and customization.

With a keychain in hand and a new friendship in the works, I established with Michael what would become an incredible partnership over the years by amplifying the COACH brand in the Bay Area and establishing the JD brand in New York. We collaborated on a private shopping event and in-store photoshoots. We attended exclusive product launches, and I was given a first look at their handbag customization line and behind-the-scenes tours. I even flew out to attend a Yankee game with the team.

By taking a chance and hustling my ass off, I built a meaningful and leverageable relationship with the team at COACH. I now have many clients who are loyal to the brand and align to their values. As for me, I have more than a keychain from this iconic brand — I'm the proud owner of several vintage bags and two customized handbags. Each with a story to tell.

Don't Underestimate Your Value

In the first few months, I struggled to pitch myself and my services to potential clients. Soon, I realized that the best way to gain more clients was to understand how my current clients would explain the services that I provided. So I started asking each of them ... What kind of value did she find in what I did? What did and didn't she like about the session? Was the session too short or too long? Did I work too fast or not fast enough? What services would she want to see as a follow-up? How were my style tips?

In addition to these probing questions, I asked my clients a question that went to the heart of the JD brand, and it's a question that I continue to ask to this day. "How would you describe what I do to someone else?" What she responded with would help me to understand what aspects of the service worked for her and what didn't, and it allowed me to tailor my next pitch to another client better. If she used words like "personal shopper" to explain my work, then I knew I had missed the mark. If she used words like "therapy" or "rebrand," then I knew I was headed in the right direction.

Running my business effectively involved huge learning curves for me. I grossly underestimated the job scope and time it took for a full on-site styling. As it turns out, every woman describes their closet smaller than it really is. Most women have clothes that are stashed in small areas of the closet that they forget about until I am there. Most women's closets are more than the three or four walls attached to their bedroom. There are other clothes stored in other parts of the house as well. Asking to see her clothes is like opening Pandora's box.

Initially, I had no idea how much I should promise. What I thought would be easy to do sometimes proved to be too hard to deliver. I also completely underestimated the amount of time behind the scenes I needed to complete the project, and I wasn't prepared for the pure physical exhaustion my clients experienced as they tried on each piece of clothing they owned.

I had no clue how physically and emotionally draining these sessions would ultimately be for me too. I organized, folded and sorted clothes while piling others in bags to carry out to my car for donations. On top of that, I also dealt with some of these women's deepest personal insecurities and struggles. After five hours of intense work, I was usually knocked out for the rest of the day and night. I felt like a therapist who needed to understand how to compartmentalize client stories from my daily life, and boy was it exhausting.

All that aside, what I walked away with was the most addictive feeling that I had had since curbside counseling. Watching a woman transform with confidence in herself and style was pretty powerful. Her stories would replay in my mind and I would go home hyper-focused on what her needs were moving forward and things I could do to help. I anxiously awaited her first text of her latest outfit.

My first paid styling job brought on some serious anxiety. For me, asking for money and placing a value on my services was, and still is, the most difficult part of running a company. I believe that part of the reason for this challenge is that when I take on a client, I don't take on her project based on how much I will make. So, if I'm not driven by money, asking for it is even harder.

Asking for money and placing a value on my services was, and still is, the most difficult part of running a company.

However, I learned quickly that you can't run a business if you don't make money. As I struggled with a bit of imposter syndrome, I knew that for the only way for me to feel confident with my fees was to find out what the market demanded. This proved to be difficult to figure out. Many stylists kept their fees private. Even their business structures weren't clear. Some included affiliations and commissions; other kept it separate. From the little information I could find, price ranges varied greatly from $25 to $1,500 per hour for comparable services.

I knew that if I priced my fees too low, my services wouldn't be taken seriously. But if I priced too high, I feared that I wouldn't secure enough clients. On one side, I realized that the worst a client could say would be "no" or possibly she would try to negotiate the price. On the other side, if I didn't see the value in myself, how could I ask her to believe in me?

Over time, my pricing set itself organically. The more my services and bespoke process was fine-tuned, the better I was at setting my fees. It is important to remember, if you run a business, that your fees aren't just for the time and energy you spend on a specific project. They are for all the experience, training and network that you bring to the table. Once you fully understand your value in the market, then and only then can you set a revenue bar commensurate with your experience and expertise, and begin to weed out potential clients or customers who just aren't ready to work with you or purchase your products or services.

Setting the Course

My company was expanding rapidly. I had full-time and part-time employees, several dedicated consultants and an on-call network of stores and designers. But the right people alone wouldn't ensure my success. I realized that the success of my business would hinge on the implementation of a strategic business plan. It was essential that I established a framework and foundation to scale effectively, strategically and with intention. JD's success hinged on my ability to align the company's vision and core values with each member who joined my extended team.

The timing couldn't have been more perfect. I was hired to do an extensive project that would stretch my ability to maintain balance in my life. All my time and energy were tapped at the end of the project, which spanned several days on-site and two weeks to complete. At the time, it was the largest wardrobe I had worked on and the first client for whom I designed and customized a personalized "by Janel Dyan" lookbook.

It took more than 15 hours on-site to go through each piece of her wardrobe, give style tips and assemble outfit after outfit to show her how to build complete looks. By day two, I realized that my client was struggling to remember all the tips I shared. Not only was she overwhelmed with how to wear all the pieces in her closet, but she forgot the style tips for how to put outfits together after I left. And, if I'm being honest, so did I. How could we make the decisions and the learning more "sticky" over time? It was a question that I needed to answer.

At this point in the evolution of my business, the average JD client had between 500 and 1,500 pieces of clothing in her closet, and I was managing approximately seven clients at the time. My client base wasn't slowing down, and I could no longer recall the wardrobes of each client like I wanted to. I started to consider building my clients a printed, customized lookbook — something beautiful and leather-bound, with an outfit per page and with their own pieces laid out with handwritten notes for each.

My team will tell you that I have high expectations for myself, for them and for the services we deliver. Just like many ideas I have, what I thought would be a straightforward lookbook turned out to be extremely time intensive. But it was important to me and to my company, so I took it slow and methodically.

First, I took pictures of all the new outfits and garments I suggested for my client. Next, I manually cropped out the background, adjusted the lighting and then laid out the ensemble with options for accessories, a handbag, shoes and overcoat. After printing each look, I laid them out on my kitchen table and rearranged by season and event. When it was all in order, the final lookbook was bound and ready for handwritten notes and personal comments about when and where to wear what. The final product was stunning, and when the client opened it up, it was a great way to celebrate the work we had done together.

The lookbooks that were created were a great additional product to support my services, but I quickly found out that the process wasn't worth the price. I had a product that was cool, but truth be told, as soon as it was printed, it was going out of date. For clients who made frequent wardrobe purchases and/or donations, the entire lookbook could be out of date within months. To make it worth my time and my client's investment, I had to go digital.

Aligning Your Passion to the Market

I went out to the market — to my competitors and to every fashion and style consultation service I could find — and looked to see if there was an app that allowed us to capture a wardrobe and lay out outfits with notes and custom details, but there was nothing that accomplished exactly what I wanted.

I thought about creating my own app, but instead of investing money into building something for an unknown market (i.e., I had no idea if there was significant demand for what I wanted to offer), I tried to find an option that would get me most of the way there. My team discovered StickyAlbums, which was a great place to start. This app was built for photographers to share their work with individual clients, but it had the core functions I needed for my business. It allowed me to create a customized mobile portfolio of a client's wardrobe and looks through images. In the beginning, it took hours to build each look in PowerPoint, but within a few months, I was able to manage each piece and build multiple looks in much less time. More importantly, we tailored the outfit based on the true size of the client so that what she saw in the mirror would look the same on her image in the lookbook.

This lookbook streamlined my process and allowed me to work remotely and quickly. I could also track what outfits a client wore versus the ones she passed on. I could track user data to fine tune my questions during our appointments and have discussions about what images were clicked on most, how effective the album was based on how many times she opened it and what pieces she wasn't loving. Ultimately, our conversations about buying new clothes, releasing others or cost-per-wear (CPW) were simple and logical.

Cost-per-wear isn't just about how much an item costs divided by the number of times you wear it. There are several factors that need to be taken into account, such as whether an item is seasonal or can be worn year-round, can it withstand rain and snow, will it need dry cleaning service or have shoe repair costs like re-heeling or suede protection? CPW has also helped my clients to curb impulse buys, as it established a more deliberate mindset in retail purchasing.

Not only was I able to scale my client base quickly and better remember each client's wardrobe and past looks, I was able to give white-glove service in real-time without having to be on-site. Each client's experience was seamless, easy and a fun visual of their looks to share with their friends.

Needless to say, the JD digital lookbook became a true differentiator in the market I served.

At Muse's End

The connections I made in the early days of wading into the fashion industry continued to be invaluable for me, and good things kept happening because of the support from the KUT from the Kloth team. We would collaborate on several KUT-sponsored events and they even hosted exclusive live fireside chats with their community on Facebook, sharing tips on what KUT pieces to wear for the season and how to style my favorite pieces. As a perk, I offered to do a give-away of a free KUT-inspired customized digital lookbook to a few of their top customers. When KUT was looking to promote their new line of jeans at the local Nordstrom, they offered to promote my services as their Style Muse. The brand recognition was massive for JD.

On a trip to New York, I was lucky enough to catch dinner with my brother at a trendy new restaurant in Harlem. As we sipped wine, ate our appetizers and caught up with our lives, we were politely interrupted. A well-dressed, middle-aged man asked, "Are you, by chance, Janel Dyan?" I nodded and he continued, "I wanted to tell you that I really like your work." He had been sitting with his daughter and wife, and when he recognized me, they looked me up on Instagram. Turns out it was Mitchell Quaranta, CEO, President of Swat Fame, Inc., the parent company of KUT from the Kloth.

It was the *ultimate* validation for me.

At a certain point, however, the scales tipped in my relationship with this important partner. My company was growing and validation doesn't pay the mortgage, so I needed to evolve the relationship or move on. I loved working with the team at KUT, but I needed to get paid in dollars, not just free jeans. I proposed a new relationship that involved me getting compensated for my time and services; unfortunately, they didn't see the value at the time. It was then that I realized that the disconnect wasn't just about the paycheck. I found that my work with KUT meant I had to be on Instagram hourly, post blogs daily, and constantly pose in pictures and take selfies. It required a lot of my time and was overwhelming. I started noticing that what I really loved to do wasn't about *me* — it wasn't about Janel, but about JD ... wasn't about my sense of style but about the stories and styles of other women I could help. Yet, everything I was doing for KUT, on the outside, was all about me — a social media personality that felt self-absorbed to me. My activities and the brand I was building on Instagram no longer felt aligned to the company I wanted to build. So, I called KUT, said thank you to the woman who had brought me onboard, and walked away.

Being a style muse had given me a platform to share my life, my stories, my style and ultimately establish my brand as a stylist. It was an experience I am still grateful for ... a stepping stone to where I was headed.

Balance Doesn't Exist, Non-Negotiables Do

In the beginning, I sacrificed a lot to make my company successful. It took long hours, late nights, distracted conversations and missed activities. Work-life balance, I came to learn, was not about balance at all. In fact, I don't think balance exists and shouldn't be a goal we strive to hit. The concept that, in one day, we can wake up to enjoy breakfast with our kids, work out, run a business, catch up with a friend, keep the house running, have dinner at home with our partners and, at the end of the day, get a good night's sleep is impossible.

In fact, I think that the quest for "balance" holds us back as women more than it helps us.

However, there are parts of my life that I would not sacrifice as I built my business and, to this day, still don't. I call these my "non-negotiables." I stick to them, no matter what, because my non-negotiables give me the greatest perspective in life and keep me grounded.

I didn't start out with a pre-defined list of non-negotiables. I had many "it would be nice if I don't miss" events on my list, such as picking up the boys at school, having dinner with them or watching them at soccer practice. But it was only when I was faced with having to make a hard decision that it became crystal clear what the difference was between a "nice to have" and a "non-negotiable." And, to be honest, I didn't always learn what mattered when I sacrificed something important the *first* time. But when it happened for the second time, there was no question what I needed to do.

My most important non-negotiable came to light in 2015.

During my second trip to New York Fashion Week (NYFW), I sat on the floor of my hotel room — alone, tired, hungry, physically exhausted and with blisters on my feet. I held the phone in one hand and held my forehead with the other. I felt like a complete failure as a mom. I was 3,000 miles away from a very important moment I had promised myself and the boys I wouldn't miss again ... a birthday. Months earlier, JJ had turned 10 while I was standing alone in Lincoln Center and this particular evening, Evan was turning 7.

I can still hear Evan's broken-hearted little voice coming through the phone, asking me when I was coming home. He didn't understand why I couldn't be there and why I had broken my promise to never miss a birthday. He begged me to be there when he woke up the next morning. Each word he said broke my heart. In that moment, I had an honest debate with myself. *"What more was I willing to sacrifice? What moments in my life would I be willing to give up?"* A line had to be drawn ... and it was. The next morning, I took the first flight home and made it in time for school pick up.

My sons' birthdays happen to fall precisely during the two bi-annual NYFW events. One of my non-negotiables is that I will not miss my sons' birthdays. To this day, even when incredible opportunities have presented themselves — no matter how tempted I am to go back — NYFW is no longer in the cards for me.

Failure IS Success

My biggest failures have given me the most powerful "aha" moments and provided such sudden clarity from out of nowhere. That clarity has become the disruption I have needed to make massive change in my life and work, and it has forced JD to pivot directions. With time, I shifted my mindset and changed how I defined the word "failure." For me, failure became the catalyst for great change.

- Honestly, I have failed so many times that I have almost lost count. Almost. Here's the current count:
- I was denied membership by six women-in-business and entrepreneurial-based organizations.

- I had seven companies straight up tell me "no" when I suggested we collaborate.
- I invested in 19 Kickstarter wearable product campaigns that bombed.
- I launched 12 services that the market did not find valuable.
- I submitted eight articles to op-ed publications that did not get picked up.
- I started two product companies that never launched.

"If you fall flat on your face, you've learned something incredibly valuable that you can take to your next venture."
- Adam Lowry, Co-Founder of Method and Ripple Foods

Respect Is Worth More than Revenue

I learned — the hard way — how essential it is to set clear expectations and to provide transparency for my clients. Initially, I made the mistake of shying away from the hard conversations early in the relationship.

Things had started out great with a client and her husband, for whom I was leading a major closet overhaul. They were both open to change and my team enjoyed being a part of it all. We were working closely for several months and things were going so smoothly that when I started creeping over the original scope of work, I missed the opportunity to reset and circle back with them to discuss our contract and billing fees. To be fair, I still wasn't billing as many hours as I should have but we were beyond the scope of the original contract and neither party brought it up. I was having too much fun, and asking for money has never come easily for me.

However, after two more months of extensive additional work, the project was coming to an end. Though the clients were aware that there would be additional fees included, the final bill was met with shock, frustration and disappointment. I took a big hit to cover the costs of my team's efforts and I learned a huge lesson. Over-communicating when it comes to contracts, services and billing is always the best choice. The invoice was never paid, not even in part, and I lost a client and a relationship.

"Your most unhappy customers are your greatest source for learning."

- Bill Gates

Clear, ample, respectful and timely communication matters on both sides of the client-provider relationship. I once fired a client based on the way she was treating my employees. Every woman who works with the JD team is an extension of me. Our values, our ethics and the respect we demand is a non-negotiable. When I choose to work with someone, they must respect everyone on the team. This particular client, however, was dismissive, rude, demeaning and engaged completely differently with my colleagues when I was not in the room. I was surprised and disappointed, and simply couldn't tolerate this behavior from our client. So I let her know that our services would no longer be available to her. Although my business was small at the time and the client would have delivered significant revenue, walking away was my only choice.

Building a Roadmap That Begins with WHY

So, I began to read *Behind the Cloud* by Marc Benioff, Chairman, co-Chief Executive Officer and Founder of Salesforce. In his book, I learned about Marc's established framework called the V2MOM, which helps companies build a template for growth and alignment based on their vision and values. V2MOM stands for vision, values, methods, obstacles and measures.

During the same summer I read Marc's book, I had a team of four incredible women at JD and we took that model and used it to establish our first JD version of a V2MOM. It was my goal to share where I wanted to go, to create a roadmap of how to get there and to bring my team into alignment with the full vision of the company.

To explain a bit more, the original JD V2MOM that was built over that weekend can be found page 118. Though the company's vision has evolved, and the tactics have strengthened, at its core, the values of the company have never wavered.

Establishing JD's V2MOM brought such clarity for each team member and unification among us. Like a ship at sea, we focused more on the light far away than the distractions of what was around us. It's tempting to chase the next contract or paycheck. But I discovered early on that the value of my key clients and partners wasn't so much about cash flow for our business as it was about feedback they provided about how we were doing. Each engagement, big or small, was a critical learning opportunity, helping us to grow and network. Our V2MOM kept us focused on our long-term goals when the short-term gains were so enticing.

Like a ship at sea, we focused more on the light far away than the distractions of what was around us.

In fact, during fall 2016, I was tempted to veer from my strategies and values because big projects and big money are *always* enticing … at first. I was given the potential opportunity to work with a team of a well-known East Coast developer. The project would include private

THE JD V2MOM

Vision

As fashion and brand advisors serving New York, Chicago and San Francisco, Janel Dyan helps clients develop a deeper understanding of themselves and the power they possess to disrupt the marketplace and bring positive change within their community.

Values

1. The Client's Why (Stories Matter)
2. Seamless Experience
3. Unquestionable Integrity
4. Brutal Honesty
5. Disrupt the Market
6. Beyond Us

Methods

1. **Inspire New Clients:** Attract and sign new corporate and high-net-worth personal clients. Network and ask for referrals.

2. **Maximize Client Time:** Face-to-face interactions with clients drive loyalty and revenues. Scale remote interactions and communication.
3. **The JD Brand:** Be the expert. Tighten web/social presence. Lead panels. Challenge beliefs. Make statements at events and associate with key partners, events and brands.
4. **Disrupt with Technology and Data:** Build and deploy a digital app to connect with clients from anywhere. Collect and analyze client, industry and operational data to define what will be. Own the trends.
5. **Beyond Us:** Integrate social good with key partnerships, clients, employees and brand.
6. **Partner and Resource for Flexible Growth:** Build a bench for all services and on-call talent in all three key regions. Have resources ready to expand (and retract) in an instant. Invest in them to *be* JD. Find mentors.
7. **Manage the Business:** Bill and pay accurately and on time. Stay profitable. Prepare the infrastructure and operations for long-term success. Invest in team JD.

(continued)

Obstacles

1. **Inspire New Clients:** Locking down one large corporate client takes time. Given that the JD client believes in our WHY, are there enough high-net-worth JD clients in the Bay Area? Can we support clients outside the Bay Area?

2. **Maximize Client Time:** Client time comes in waves — how do we prioritize? People pay for JD — how do we fairly charge for other stylists? Women get hooked by JD — how do we manage their experience and face time with Janel without going beyond their spending comfort levels? Most clients don't have a set budget.

3. **The JD Brand:** How do we keep up with trends from the New York, London, Paris and Milan Fashion Weeks, and incorporate/disrupt it for the Bay Area? How valuable is the web for our specific clients? How can we grow the brand without losing authenticity? Is the app a key piece of our brand?

4. **Disrupt with Technology and Data:** We're not technology experts. Will people love the app or is a second or third version/release needed? How do I get unique industry data? What data are we looking for?

5. **Beyond Us:** What are the right organizations to give back to? Do we go with focus (bigger impact) or wide (touch more)? Who are the key influencers who can help JD play in the arena? Who can we engage to be the brand champion to grow this arm of business with Janel?

6. **Partner and Resource for Flexible Growth:** Can we cover something as big as Dreamforce should it scale beyond our proposal? How do we maintain the high standards of JD with part-time people? What measurables need to be added to help trigger action?

7. **Manage the Business:** Billing and invoicing aren't fun and inspiring. How much do you invest in infrastructure before consistent growth?

Measurables

1. **Inspire New Clients:** Close Dreamforce, secure 10 new clients, receive five referrals and complete 20 repeat engagements.

2. **Maximize Client Time:** 75 percent on-site billing

3. **The JD Brand:** Attend New York or London Fashion Week. Rebrand/update website. Lead four panels. Land three articles for print/social media release.

4. **Disrupt with Technology and Data:** App rollout. Four quarterly trend reports.

5. **Beyond Us:** Secure $300,000 in client donations. Spend 50 hours of company donated time.

6. **Partner and Resource for Flexible Growth:** Two employees. Two partner events.

7. **Manage the Business:** Zero late client billing

styling events with some of the region's wealthiest families, potential fundraising partnerships, brand alignment with influential designers and a huge opportunity to grow my client list. While this partnership could have put JD on the map with a massive new demographic, I realized something when I took a moment to be honest with myself. Not only would I have over-stretched myself to cover the East Coast and deliver services successfully, there was a drastic conflict between my values and the developer's. I couldn't sign on.

Because I had a document like a V2MOM and alignment with my team, declining this opportunity was it was one of the easiest decisions I ever made.

CHAPTER 6

The Intersection of Fashion and Technology

Around this time, crowdfunding was taking off and wearables (i.e., wearable technology products) were among the hottest trends. Companies like Kickstarter and Indiegogo became platforms for entrepreneurs to quickly share their ideas and launch a campaign for investments from all over — all before ever creating or selling a single thing.

I would spend late nights scrolling through all the different types of pitches, which typically consisted of a video from the founder and a demo of the product, a quick website with photos and mission statement, early reviews, their goals and reasons for starting the company and what my investment would provide me. There were levels of investments and perks for each level. In a way, it reminded me of my days at JAMDAT, doing quality assurance for new mobile video games.

I was fascinated by what people were trying to bring to market and *why* they felt that someone would invest in it. Almost immediately, I noticed that wearables were getting more and more traction. I supported several different campaigns that focused on fashion wearables for women. If I thought that I would possibly wear a product and use it, I invested in it.

I was intrigued by products such as:

- Bracelets with the ability to change the design and color based on your outfit
- Necklaces that doubled as an alert button should you get lost or need help
- A ring that could monitor your sleep patterns
- A jacket that was retroreflective to hide your face and protect your privacy when captured on camera.

Though many of the products I invested in never made it to market, let alone my doorstep, the products that did make it were pretty cool. (Today, of the 15 products I supported, there are only two that have remained in business, proving that a hot market can still be a difficult and competitive market.)

A Perfectly Timed Partnership

In spring of 2015, I stood with fellow parents in the school's multi-purpose room for a pizza party, watching the kids run around playing various games. Within a few minutes, I noticed the watch that one of the dads was wearing. Black with a square face bordered in slate grey, with simple digital numbers. I walked over to get a closer look.

With a smile on his face, he pulled up his sleeve. It was the first time I had heard of or seen a Pebble Time smartwatch. I was instantly thrown back in time to my high school days — the watch looked like it was designed as an ode to vintage Atari.

I was well aware of the growing smartwatch market. My husband, who has always been an early adapter and loyal customer of Apple, was one of the first to buy the first-generation Apple Watch when it came out. Dave loved it and, though I could see why he loved it, I just couldn't see myself wearing what everyone else was wearing.

I tried on the Pebble Time.

"What do you think?" the father asked.

With a large watch face and bands that don't accommodate smaller wrists, it was clear to me that these smartwatches were designed with only men in mind.

"Pebble is missing a huge market. Women won't wear this," I replied.

I proceeded to tell him that while I thought the watch was different in its design and UI (user interface) than the Apple Watch, it screamed "techie." Lacking a sleek and elegant design, the watch gave me no reason to buy it. For most women, a watch needs to be an extension of her current style and accessories game. This watch fell short.

However, what I did like about the watch was the price. At a much lower price point than similar products, this was a smartwatch that *everyone* could buy at a time when everyone wanted to be a part of this exciting new industry — especially in Silicon Valley. I also like that Pebble would give those who were not Apple fans an opportunity to make a statement and wear its competitor.

The feedback was heard and, most importantly, respected. By the end of the night, Jeff would introduce me to KR, a senior executive at Pebble, who would become an instrumental mentor during this time. She taught me about the wearables landscape, explored areas in the market that wearables had yet to capitalize on and helped me redefine what direction JD wanted to go in. KR would also introduce me to the company's partnership team and, before long, a collaboration between JD and Pebble was established. The focus was on enhancing their brand within among women.

I spent the next three months providing mini-blogs and style images, styling product marketing campaigns at New York Fashion Week (during my very last trip there before I got clarity about family birthdays and "non-negotiables") and at the Outside Lands Music and Arts Festival. The collaboration also included lifestyle photoshoots along the Bay Area coast, in iconic locales and homes of the rich and famous. JD would also consult as the style advisor during photoshoots for digital product marketing. From lifestyle articles about "disconnecting while staying connected" and blogs about how to start a trend and wear a Pebble, I became Pebble's exclusive style and brand consultant that summer.

Wearables in New York

When it came to talking about wearables to women, one of the biggest complaints that I heard was the lack of style options. What women choose to accessorize an outfit with can change daily. What we put on our wrist, around our necks, in our ears and on our fingers instantly starts conversations or establishes credibility among us. And while multiple designers either collaborated with technology companies (Tory Burch and FitBit, Hermes and Apple iWatch) or integrated technology into their products (Kate Spade's chargeable handbags, Rebecca Minkoff's chargeable keychains), the products that I felt the strongest about were ones that solved a need and didn't look like a wearable at all. Ringly (a smartring that pairs with your phone to send you customized alerts through a beautiful black oynx cocktail ring via vibrations and color changes) and Qbracelet (a fashionable iPhone charging bracelet in gold, silver or gunmetal) are two great examples.

Pebble's Time Round begins shipping this weekend, hits stores too

Justin Herrick
November 5, 2015

Best Buy Pebble target Time Round

The products that I brought to New York were tremendously

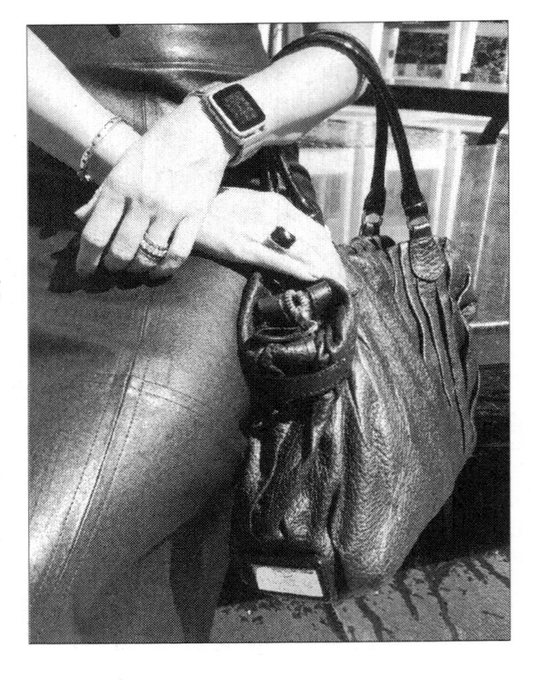

valuable in establishing JD as the expert in buying behaviors and attitudes of executive women in the Bay Area and how those insights translate to the development and marketing of wearable technologies. Each visit, I would pack several of these pieces to wear as a way to control the conversation I wanted to have. Unique and bold, these items gave me the chance to then share my work, the digital product I was working on, what actually sold within my client market, fashion movements (like social causes, environmental awareness and inclusivity), details about the markets JD played in and global consumer trends that mattered to my business.

Every time I walked back into COACH, Kate Spade, Donna Karan or Intermix, I made a point to wear a new product. My focus was to bring relatively unknown products — like the Pebble — to the world of women's high fashion. My social media posts shifted from images of fashion, trending outfits, selfies and style tips to documenting my travels to New York with my newest wearable, articles about fashion versus function, blogs about brands that were at the forefront in embracing a shifting "for cause" market and op-eds on how the buying power of the Bay Area women were becoming more influential. Momentum was building.

When I traveled out to New York Fashion Week for Pebble, I spent three jam-packed days with runway shows, taking photos of the

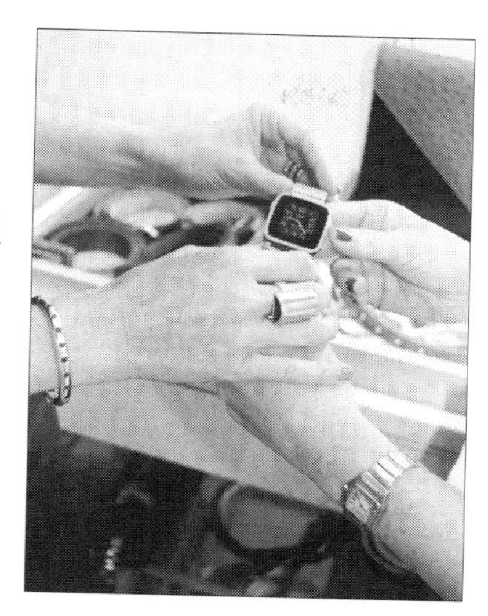

fashion on the streets, coffee meetings, afternoon style appointments and networking dinners. With the Ringly, Qbracelet and the Pebble Steel smartwatch, new doors opened up. I had the opportunity build new partnerships and secure new clients and execute a successful Pebble media collaboration.

On the concrete steps at Lincoln Center, the same steps that I had been photographed on six months earlier, two young South American fashion designers asked to take my photo. This time, it wasn't about my jacket or my outfit. Instead, it was about the wearables I was wearing.

I was living my dream — serving as the link between the Bay Area tech world and New York's world of fashion. As one executive in the retail industry told me, the JD brand is the "combination of beauty and brains." In fact, that combination is the essence of women at large.

Product-Focused, Service-Driven

At this point, the digital lookbooks that I was creating on StickyAlbums were becoming an integral part of both my private and corporate clients' deliverables. However, as the projects grew, I was extremely limited on what I could do from the back end. I was running massive Excel spreadsheets, was sharing client status reports and notes with my assistant stylists in multiple and confusing versions, and my non-billable hours were not justified by what I was bringing in. I needed to be able to quantify and streamline wardrobe digitalization, real-time digital style/looks delivery, personal styling activity and product procurement. I needed to build something to help me pull it all together and give me the data to identify the common habits and trends.

I couldn't do it alone. I didn't have the time or skills to build what I needed. The investment was going to require a massive collaboration with an outside consulting agency. I needed someone to understand who I was, why I launched my company, my vision of the product and help to discover a market that had yet to be created. I found that team in Canada.

From the first exploratory phone call with Todd and Tylor, co-founders of Denim & Steel Interactive (a digital studio in Vancouver that provides intuitive, strategy-led software and technology), I knew that I had found a partnership that was honest, authentic and completely aligned with what mattered most to us: the client's experience. Our collaboration went beyond an intuitive CRM tool. The biggest topic around the discussion of this build was about the idea of establishing an application that provided ideas of truth and trust. Hyper-focused on understanding what the human experience would be, Todd and Tylor took the helm to drive the application to a wireframe into alpha version, a blueprint for the software.

They asked me to break down what I did and how I worked with my clients. Through that discovery process, we were able to capture and document, for the first time, the repeatable processes that I used with each client — which eventually became the core of the JD Methodology.

Developing this technology tool was a strategic play and investment for the long term. The mission was to create an entire ecosystem of tools, data-driven insights, and inspirational content that would provide a platform for all women to learn about and utilize the JD Methodology — to discover their own stories, to align their style for any audience and to confidently re-brand themselves authentically.

Partnerships with Shared Values

From the start, early partnerships had to be hyper-aligned to my company values. My top priority was to stick to my core values every step of the way. Every engagement, partnership and client that JD worked with needed to share the same core values because the more alignment I could find, the better JD was able to deeply cement our own place in the marketplace, our corporate personality and the value we offered.

I found such a partnership with Shilpa Shah, the Co-Founder of Cuyana, a pioneering fashion brand in the changing e-commerce and retail spaces. Cuyana successfully marries luxury-level branding with premium quality apparel and accessories, offering "fewer, better things" to women at accessible price points. During the time of the "fast fashion" boom, Cuyana's core values of conscious consumption and sustainability resonated deeply with me. Furthermore, with philanthropic partners like H.E.A.R.T. (part of the Violence Intervention Program), Cuyana was dedicated to enriching the lives of women by bringing new life to recycled styles customers no longer needed.

This was the first brand that aligned with JD's Beyond Us program, and I couldn't have been more excited.

My brother introduced the two of us. He and Shilpa had met on a flight across the country and spent a few hours talking about the retail industry, her company, the current market trends and the product that I was building. By the time they landed, Shilpa had offered to meet with me, look at the digital app I was building and provide honest feedback. She jumped on several calls with Todd and Tylor to help flesh out the key features and user experience. She even met with me at her office, to map out where my product could solve her market gaps.

Most importantly, Shilpa believed in what I was doing and gave me unique opportunities to grow my brand. Shilpa and Cuyana hosted several private events for my clients, invited me to join VIP shopping opportunities and personally introduced me to a room full of professional women. Shilpa selflessly gave me her time, mentorship and her company's brand to help launch mine. To this day, her friendship and partnership are precious to me.

Returning to the Office

In September 2016, a friend called and invited me to join her for a private brunch with one of the top designers in the world. It was a "pinch me, I'm dreaming" opportunity to sit with someone ranked among the *Forbes* Top 100 Most Powerful Women in the World and included in *Time Magazine*'s Time 100 as an icon.

I was standing on the blacktop at my sons' school when the phone rang. I was standing next to my husband, with music playing and children running from the slides to go play a game of "wall ball" when I asked her what the date was for this once-in-a-lifetime event. My heart skipped a beat. I said I'd get back to her, then hung up and shared the news with Dave. It was during New York Fashion Week and it was on Evan's birthday. I turned around to find the boys and made the simple choice to decline the invitation. Not only was Evan's birthday a non-negotiable, I had begun to feel that JD no longer wanted to just exist in the world of fashion and wearables. It was another crossroads.

A few weeks prior, I began working with Suzanne DiBianca, the then Chief Philanthropy Officer at Salesforce.org, an incredible woman who is determined to solve some of the world's greatest challenges in education, workforce development and global sustainability. While building her looks for her upcoming trip to the World Economic Forum, she offered to help me in growing my company. So, I made a call and pitched Suzanne the idea of hosting "JD Office Hours" for women at Salesforce.

"Absolutely, how many women do you want me to invite?"

Section 3

A BRAND NEW ERA OF TRUST

"Marketing is no longer about the stuff that you make but about the stories you tell."

- Seth Godin

Behind the Scenes: The Show Must Go On

With 15 days to go until to my first Dreamforce, the team was executing brilliantly. The style pulls were underway at both Nordstrom and Neiman Marcus, I had met with each client and the product deliveries were beginning to show up from New York. At the time, I was simultaneously working with 12 corporate clients for Dreamforce, as well as two other private clients — so to say I was exhausted would be an understatement.

After another 12-hour day, I sat on the counter with my feet up on the island and a glass of wine in my hand, admiring a beautiful bouquet of blood orange calla lilies sitting in the middle of my dining table, a thank you gift from my client. Dave was cooking dinner as I gave him a progress report on the pilot program.

To buy us some time to talk, we started a pre-dinner snack game with our boys. The game consisted of the boys running in a circle around the house and then grabbing a small piece of apple or chicken while sprinting under my legs (I was still sitting on the kitchen counter, with my toes balanced on the island) before I could touch them with my hand.

On the fourth run, one of the boys decided to use my legs as a gate and lift them up to run under. My legs were knocked off the ledge and I remember seeing my feet up in the air over my head. I fell onto my neck, slamming directly on the hardwood floor. I tried to catch my breath while hearing myself gasping for air and trying desperately to say "I'm OK" to the kids. Dave bent over to hold my neck in place, and I kept thinking to myself, *"Please let me be okay. I can't let this stop me. I have Dreamforce to finish!"*

I was told by the doctors that I was "lucky" to have only the ligament pulled off the bone in my neck and that the concussion's side effects may be felt for a few months. The headaches were rough, and my short-term memory was nonexistent. As much as I needed to rest, I had no choice but to push on. There was no failure ... no opting out. I wanted this huge career opportunity to be a huge success, and my clients didn't need to know I was injured.

The show had to go on.

CHAPTER 7

Disrupting the Corporate Style

Suzanne came through and, together, we built out a guest list of 20 women to attend my first "office hours." The idea for the event was to give a presentation on what trends were being seen on the New York Fashion Week runways and how to bring them into the world of Silicon Valley.

In typical fashion, I had just "sold" a concept that I had absolutely no idea how to pull off ... but I knew where to start.

Finding Yoda

With her petite build, shiny black hair, bright red lipstick and jean jacket draped over her shoulders accenting a 1940s-inspired dress, Maggie's style, passion and personality were a breath of fresh air. Unique, bold, vintage and engaging — her love of fashion went beyond just retail.

I met Maggie, by chance, at the Intermix store in Soho, NYC, during a rainstorm one fall day. I was with a friend and I was shopping for a new pair of jeans, as I had just ripped my current pair in a location that wasn't all too flattering. As most of us have experienced, there are times when the sales associate who works with you may not understand your style — missing the mark on the items they pull for the dressing room. Maggie wasn't one of them, which surprised me, because our individual styles were clearly very different. Her ability to ask me exploratory questions was impressive, and I ended up with a pair of jeans that not only fit amazingly well, but were a brand I would have never thought of. What I loved most about Maggie from the start was that she was honest with me. She focused on what worked for me, and though I'm sure she could have sold more pieces if she wanted to, I felt that she cared more about what I *would* wear vs what I *could* wear.

Being assisted by Maggie was an experience so positive that she came to mind when I started working on the "office hours" project. I trusted her honesty and knew I could learn a lot from her. So, I flew out (using as many accrued miles as I could!) to spend the day with Maggie. With no preconceived notion that I would be purchasing anything, she graciously offered to give me a crash course into the world of high-fashion retail.

She taught me about brands, designers, trends, size conversions and the looks that her typical clientele would gravitate toward. She explained the drastic sizing differences between brands in the U.S. and which ones to take a size up and ones to size down. She explained the conversions of the European sizing and how that correlated with the average American woman. She walked me through the "hottest up-and-coming designers" to hit the runways, brands that were losing their grip on the market, and trends for the Millennial and Gen X markets.

She taught me how to pronounce designers' names properly. She even allowed me to record her pronouncing brands such as Givenchy, Hermes, L'Agence and Louis Vuitton. It was essential for me that I knew the correct pronunciations when working with clients. Though I knew all about the brands, styles and trends, being able to pronounce the name was important when working with a client!

Success for my business meant that I had to become an expert, which meant that I *actually* had to become *the* expert. Maggie was my Yoda.

The establishment of the JD brand depended my willingness to learn.

Maggie was able to break down and describe how New York Fashion Week really worked. She educated me on the top five trends for each season, and shared the story behind each look and each designer's collection shown on the runway. Each design was unique — each a piece of art in motion, telling a story on its way down the catwalk. Listening to her characterization of the season — going into great detail about trends like "Leather and Lace," "Rockstar Chic" and "Pure Decadence" — I began to see fashion in a new light and to appreciate it in a way that I hadn't before. And the timing was perfect, because my vision of the "office hours" event required truly delighting a group of 20 Bay Area women with a style consultation like nothing they ever imagined.

Runway to Real Way

With new knowledge and confidence (thanks to Maggie), I was ready to really plan my event. The goal was to be able to collaborate in building 12 key outfits that the Bay Area executive woman could incorporate into her professional brand. These looks would represent the season's trends, the newest designers, designers who supported social causes and easy, classic "already have in your closet" basics. Maggie challenged me to bring some edgy New York style back, and I shared what looks would definitely *not* make it on the streets of Silicon Valley. With each outfit, we created transitional pieces to go from day to night and took photos when each were completed.

We also understood that the way for this to be successful, the way to establish myself as the style advisor, was to not *only* have all 12 pieces

but another rack with additional fun styles. I'd have these pieces shipped to my office to be on-hand during the JD Office Hours. With more than $30,000 worth of merchandise, Maggie took a big chance on me and set up my first consignment account.[1]

So, how would the JD Office Hours work? The goal of this event was to guide the women in learn how to build looks, allow them to ask questions about designers and have the opportunity to purchase apparel and accessories on the spot. I presented the 12 looks and additional items. I talked through the recent trends. I provided tips, like ways to increase their Cost Per Wear (CPW) by showing how to mix and match. Most importantly, I made it real and more visceral for them by having these items there so they could touch and feel everything. They could try on things on and I could help identify the right sizing and true fit. This was so much more than a catalog party, and it was held at their workplace, where they felt comfortable and where they were in the midst of the very contexts of what they might want to convey when they walked into the building each morning, showing off their own stories through their individual styles. Collectively, they

1 A consignment account in luxury retail is when a store sends a selection of curated pieces directly to you to shop through at your leisure. Your credit card is kept on file and is only charged for anything kept.

all represented one corporate brand and several individual personalities, which are brands in their own rights.

All the while, Maggie was on hand, pulling sizing, providing advice and placing orders for the women. To wrap it all up, I created a digital lookbook for each woman to take with them after the presentation. JD proved to be one of Maggie's (and Intermix's) most lucrative partners that year.

Back in the Office

I had left the corporate world more than 10 years prior, but that day — standing in that conference room, exploring fashion for the workplace with a dozen other successful women —was the day I knew I had returned. And this time, I was a completely different brand. I was standing where I knew I wanted to be.

During the previous two years, I tested the markets, styled clients from New York, Chicago, Dallas and San Francisco, worked with brands and emerging designers, re-established myself many times, rebranded and redefined my company over and over, finetuned my services, and developed products. I had been a style muse, a blogger, a stylist and a wearables advocate. I'd done countless Closet Rehabs, collaborated as a style consultant for companies and launched a philanthropic platform called Beyond Us.

And now, I had become a brand that I couldn't have imagined but that was exactly what I wanted to be: Janel Dyan, expert brand and style advisor in the Bay Area for women in the corporate workforce. JD was now working with powerful women, learning their narratives, talking about style and teaching them the value of investing in their professional brand. I believed, and still do, that women in leadership have the biggest potential to disrupt global markets in every industry.

Women in leadership have the biggest potential to disrupt global markets in every industry.

What's Hot, What's Not

With Dreamforce '16 coming up, I headed back into Salesforce to host another JD Office Hours. This session was specifically about a woman's style during the world's largest technology conference. I kept my focus on the top trends of the season and how to incorporate these looks into a style that could be fun and functional.

The criteria wouldn't be all that simple. Function needed to be just as important as fashion — not something easily found.

The women would need to be comfortable to get through long days on their feet, at times walking several miles a day. They needed to have a handbag or backpack that could hold a variety of tech gadgets, as well as their laptop. They needed outfits that allowed them to get from day meetings to client dinners without changing. And, of course, true to the stereotypical "hoodies, jeans and runners" of the Bay Area, I created elevated "hoodie" looks for them when a corporate hoodie was required. It was important to me that they would be able to dress for their audience and yet still be themselves in style.

I presented more wearables, chargers, backpacks. I found the most comfortable flats that could be worn when walking from place to place — easily storable in their bag. I suggested skirts, jackets and trousers that were breathable, should the weather turn hot, and heels that were as blister-proof as possible. I brought skinny jeans to pair with flats and a hoodie that could easily switch from day to night by throwing the hoodie in a bag and throwing on a leather jacket for dinner.

At the appointment, a few women stayed behind to learn more about my story and my growth strategy for 2016. My vision was to establish myself as the go-to strategic style and brand advisor for women leadership in corporations like Salesforce. I wanted to disrupt the way women approached what they wore, especially for public events, with the alignment of the personal story, redefining their professional brand and establishing a strategic alignment with the brand of the company they work for. I believed women in leadership were a company's most valuable asset; I also believed that women leaders are brand ambassadors for the bottom line of a company.

There was one woman who stayed longer than anyone else and spent time brainstorming ways she could help me. This woman, whose infectious laugh precedes her and whose compassion can be felt upon the first meeting, would become one of my biggest advocates and mentors.

Ebony and I had immediately connected over my vintage Louis Vuitton crossbody bag and the QBracelet wearable charging bracelet. She was a "techie" at heart. We bonded over the art of blending fashion with function in the world of Silicon Valley. The then SVP of philanthropy and engagement at Salesforce.org, she had established her professional brand brilliantly as one of the top executive women leaders who didn't see her work as a job ... but as a passion.

We placed her order and sent it off to Maggie in New York. Ebony had given me some great feedback and offered to help me finetune my next presentation. As I headed back to my office, I eagerly called Dave and shared what had just happened.

My brand and my services had been noticed.

A Company that Invests

In a small conference room on the 21st floor of the Salesforce tower, we sifted through Ebony's order, which had just arrived from New York. The fitting was amplified that day as Ebony had just been tapped for several high-profile speaking and media events during Dreamforce. I'll never forget the looks we put together that year — soft textures, bold plaids, asymmetrical hemlines and colors of burgundy, deep blues and camel.

By the end of our time together, I shared a quick update on the company and Ebony's eyes lit up. She wanted me to meet someone who was looking for a stylist for Dreamforce and thought I could be a perfect fit.

A few minutes later, wearing her signature Burberry trench coat, Linda walked into the room. The VP, Executive Briefing Centers and Strategic Keynote Events, she had just been tasked by Lynn Vojvodich, then EVP and Chief Marketing Officer, to hire a style consultant who could provide styling services for their key executive women who would be speaking at Dreamforce. These women had been asked to present some of the company's newest products in front of thousands of attendees and millions of people online.

I was impressed that Lynn, who was about to take maternity leave, made it a priority to invest in the women leadership at Salesforce. Many companies with whom I have met in the past had not seen the value or understood the power that a service like this can provide for their leaders. It's not just a gesture to show support and confidence in the keynote speakers, but a way to help those brand advocates refresh their personal style and build up a strong professional brand that had the possibility of aligning with the corporate brand in powerful ways. Furthermore, this was a direct nod to what Salesforce stood for — the empowerment of women and a commitment to bring more women into leadership positions.

Over the next hour, I sat across from Linda, learning about the fine details of what a keynote looked like, the past women and their styles on stage. We talked through all the details regarding what a collaboration could look like. She explained that providing their leaders with a service like mine was a way to show appreciation for all the extra work of preparation, and a way to reduce the anxiety surrounding what to wear so that each female keynoter could focus on what was most important ... her presentation.

My job would be to learn about the audiences they would need to engage with, the stages the women may be speaking on (whether it was a raised stage, if they were sitting or standing) and what a typical day-to-night looked like for her. I was there to ensure that what she wore aligned with every activity that week ... and that she exuded confidence.

The stakes were high. While I didn't have the infrastructure to handle this massive project just yet, I knew that if I got the opportunity to be a part of it, I would figure it out.

"If somebody offers you an amazing opportunity but you are not sure you can do it, say yes — then learn how to do it later."

- Richard Branson

We had talked through the concept, but the hard part was putting it down on paper.

The Pilot Proposal

It was a bold and risky move, but I knew that if given the opportunity, there would be a huge payoff. My job was to make sure that each executive's story, style and brand aligned with the product, the audience and the Salesforce brand. This pilot program had never been done before — JD could become the Style and Brand Advisor to the top female keynote executives at Dreamforce. Perhaps year after year.

Having never put together something like this before, I reached out to my network to see who could give me an idea of what the current market was for these services. Then I spent hours writing a proposal and establishing a pricing structure that I thought made sense.

The outcome was a "Dreamforce Styled" proposal. It was a *massive* undertaking for a very small consultancy, which included appointment times, tiered levels of support for each speaker, behind the scenes support, a breakdown of the fees and breadth of the styling services:

- Pre-style appointments
- Style pulls and consignment
- Sourcing and procurements
- Private fittings and tailoring
- Personalized digital lookbooks

- On-site conference support.

Now all I had to do was send the proposal. I was paralyzed by that simple click. I think I was more afraid said that she'd say "yes" than that she might say "no." Sitting on the floor next to the side of the bed and trying to hide the bright light of my laptop screen from waking anyone, I finally did it.

I hit "send" at 2:00 a.m.

The next day, I got the thumbs up. What had started as a styling opportunity turned into a strategic partnership to spearhead a pilot program that would become the missing link between the style of the woman and the brand of the company. I threw everything I had at this project. I called in every favor, every contact and every mentor to launch this project. This project was the furthest I had ever pushed myself and the biggest reach I had ever promised, but there was no doubt in my mind I could execute. I knew that to deliver, I needed a team to be on top of everything and stay two steps ahead of the game.

Build a Team of Experts

Seamless execution can't be done alone. My team would agree that my level of expectation for what I do and the services I provide is, at times, beyond what most believe is achievable.

I first met with Nordstrom to establish a partnership for private styling events, off-site styling assistance and consignment opportunities. I then walked into Neiman Marcus and leveraged my collaboration with Nordstrom to build a partnership and consignment account. I knew I needed dedicated dressing rooms for dozens of appointments, and leveraging multiple partnerships was the only way to make it happen.

I reached out to Maggie in New York to help with additional consignments, on-call style advice and digital lookbook support. I found an incredible seamstress, Jasmine (or, as my team and clients affectionately call her, "The Magician") who could recreate any piece to fit a body with tailoring and turnaround time like none other. In fact, the night prior to our first Dreamforce event, I was determined to create a flawless silhouette and Jasmine had to open up the entire side of the dress, on the spot, to avoid the audience being distracted by the mic wires. She built in a hidden sleeve for the wires and stitched it up with the client wearing the dress!

Finally, I reached out to my friend, Mandy. A 15-year veteran in the fashion and retail industry, she had experience in directing large-scale photoshoots, managing multiple projects for several big-name brands, and she was my ultimate sounding board. I asked her to join me as my senior style consultant and on-site manager during the week of the event.

Within eight days, I established partnerships with five retail stores, a coveted tailor, three in-store dedicated stylists, three runners to be on-call during the conference, two on-site assistant stylists, one remote style consultant in New York and a senior project manager.

Then I fell off my kitchen counter. I've never been so grateful to have a team around me.

Twelve hours after my accident, Mandy was sitting on the floor in my office, building out a strategic plan to step in and help me run the operations of the project. We spent all day creating a master spreadsheet from all my handwritten notes on my clients, appointments that had been booked and outlines noting all the support needed to execute the services to be delivered.

The next night, she came back over to keep working. With Maggie working from New York, Mandy sitting on my floor and me in a neck brace — binders open to try and remind me what I had done — we built personalized digital lookbooks for each client's Dreamforce week and created a master binder of all the looks. We organized tailoring needs and created hairstyle/makeup inspirational boards. None of us slept that night. I found out later that Maggie was scheduled to start a new job that next day, yet without hesitation, she never tagged out on me.

Like most of that year, I lucked out so many times when it came to identifying key players in the success of my company. It just so happened that the stylist I was scheduled to meet at Nordstrom, to talk about the pilot program, was unavailable for the appointment. She was gracious enough to introduce me to a woman who would become another big asset to the growth of JD. Diana was a senior style associate and an instrumental force on the team. After the concussion, she wrote extensive notes from what I shared with her and tracked every look, every designer and every style for each of the clients. During our partnership, she would meet me at 7:00 a.m. to help prepare multiple dressing rooms of personalized pieces for the clients, worked on the days she had off, brought in great style advice during the fittings, reminded me to eat, covered my ass when I couldn't recall a client's name and stayed in the trenches with me all the way to the end.

Yet, more than anything, she embodied the same values and vision of what JD stood for. Stories mattered.

Stories mattered.

"These women are leaders in work, around their communities and at home. They trusted JD to continue to tell their story, revealing an intimate individualized style. Witnessing this natural evolution, contributing toward their self-discovery , ultimately assisted me in my own story of finding my 'why.'"

– Diana Whitcomb, Style Advisor & Private Client Services, Dallas

Within 25 days, I had 14 at-home appointments that had me driving all over the Bay, 21 in-office appointments (with bathrooms turned into make-shift dressing rooms) and 30 in-store fittings at Nordstrom and Neiman Marcus. Hundreds of pieces were pulled for each client and, during each appointment, the team would have two dressing rooms full of looks ready and waiting. Orders from NY to LA were delivered to my office to be carried throughout the city and hauled in my car for appointments and the designer clothing retailers Net-a-Porter, Intermix and Far Fetch were always on standby.

I also received nine parking tickets, tossed through multiple sleepless nights, spent countless late nights in my downstairs home office with the team (including one all-nighter on FaceTime), attended too many 4:00 a.m. tailoring sessions and dozens of 7:00 a.m. in-store appointments, and walked many miles all over San Francisco with blisters on my heels and Band-Aids that kept falling off. I can even recall the searing pain from a strained bicep when I overloaded my arms with garment bags walking the seven blocks to an in-office appointment. Even the security guards at the Union Square garage would let me park on the first floor so I would be as safe as possible when I returned after 9:00 p.m. — sometimes carrying up to $10,000 worth of retail in my arms.

I was working a million miles a minute, and I never used my accident as a reason to slow down. I knew, with my team in place, I was going to be fine. But I had to be agile and I had to adapt. My concussion prevented me from getting behind the wheel. Uber became my best friend. I piled shopping bags and garment bags into every Uber car I needed. I had them drive me to San Francisco for appointments, deliveries and even, at times, asked them to deliver the clothing without me. I jumped in the back and headed to local clients' homes to personally deliver their curated pieces (once from the window in the back seat!). My clients never knew what happened because I didn't want my concussion to draw the focus away from them. My health wasn't their problem. We just needed to deliver.

And deliver we did. The pilot program was a huge success. Every woman stepped out on stage that year with such confidence and authenticity that, in an instant, she captured her audience and established the most important emotion in winning business — their trust.

CHAPTER 8

Truth, Trust and Loyalty

With thousands of hours in closets, countless miles walked on the streets of New York and multiple corporate events under my belt, it finally became clear that there was a method to my madness. I had created a process that could be successful for all women and easily implemented within any corporation. The methodology is the missing linkage between four overlapping phenomena — our DNA and human behavior, a female-driven global consumer economy, the rise of executive women in leadership and an era when marketing is the art of storytelling.

The methodology is the missing linkage between four overlapping phenomena – our DNA and human behavior, a female-driven global consumer economy, the rise of executive women in leadership and an era when marketing is the art of storytelling.

Within our first three steps — into a room, onto a stage, in front of our most valued stakeholders — we have the power to control any narrative. Each step dictates whether we are seen as competent, knowledgeable and authentic.

"At its very core, marketing is storytelling. The best advertising campaigns take us on an emotional journey — appealing to our wants, needs and desires — while at the same time telling us about a product or service."

- Melinda Partin, Multimedia Producer and Digital Marketing Director

Women want to feel connected to a brand ... to feel that their needs are understood. They want to feel confident in their decisions and they want their decisions to inspire others to do the same. Because women relate to brands uniquely and buy differently, how we communicate with them has to be an entirely different approach.

Every woman has the power to control those first three steps. By delving into her own stories and an authentic style that reflects who she is and how she wants to be seen, she has the power to be who she wants to be. She has the power to drive the results she seeks by embracing what makes her unique.

"Storytelling offers the opportunity to talk with your audience, not at them."

- Laura Holloway, Founder and Chief of The Storyteller Agency

Failing to Capitalize on What Matters Most

I had just been retained for private style consulting by Kelly, a marketing executive at a B2B software company in Chicago. During our initial consultation, I asked Kelly what prompted her to call me. She shared that her last few presentations hadn't been well-received and that she had heard about the JD Methodology while at a marketing event in the Bay Area. She explained that her presentations weren't generating the buzz she was hoping for. So, I asked her to walk me through a typical scenario of how she gets "stage ready."

I wanted the details, starting all the way back to the moment she was asked to perform.

Her boss, two levels up, asked her to present a new product on stage to their top customers that past summer. Like most of my executive clients, she didn't have too much time to prepare. Kelly was to go onstage in three weeks' time. She had to build the talk deck, set up presentation rehearsals with her team, and swing by the venue the day prior to work with the audio/visual team on sound and lighting.

I asked my client to tell me about the first thing that crossed her mind when she heard about the assignment. *"Oh crap, what am I going to wear?"*

First, Kelly heads home and looks in her closet. She researches online, asks friends for advice and checks out social media for ideas. Next, she heads over to her favorite store, tells the sales associate about her event, tries on several outfits and purchases a look that feels right for what she needs. Her outfit may even be out of her price range, but she justifies it to herself because it's for work, and it's critical that she nails the presentation. She hangs her new clothes in her closet. Relief.

In the morning, she's back at the office building several versions of her talk deck, filling up her calendar with presentation run-throughs, and pulling a late night to keep her "real" job responsibilities from dropping. She begins to feel confident in her presentation and offers to help her team push out the social media blasts to build momentum.

However, as the big day approaches, that outfit hanging in her closet comes back into view because now, she learns that she'll be on a platform stage with steps to climb. Her audience will have a 360-degree view of her. She is speechless as she seriously questions whether her current outfit will work.

She heads back home, pulls out her outfit, throws it on and turns around several times in front of her full-length mirror as she analyzes what she looks like from every angle. She focuses on the most insecure areas of her body and begins to feel extremely vulnerable, fearing that she will be criticized by her audience.

Just like that, without even knowing it, the outfit that was sure to give Kelly the boost of confidence and credibility with her audience has suddenly become the most anxiety-inducing element of the entire event. As we all now know, if Kelly doesn't exude confidence to the audience — in her first three steps — she has failed to capitalize on what matters most ... trust.

And without trust, her company has just lost its biggest opportunity for their brand to gain a strong foothold, build deeper customer loyalty and, in turn, potential revenue.

This is precisely why corporate results are a matter of personal style.

Corporate results are a matter of personal style.

Mastering the First Three Steps

To thrive in this female-driven consumer world, female leaders should be at the forefront of all strategic decisions. These leaders need to have more than just a seat at the table. In fact, companies should work to empower these women with opportunities to be in front of the audiences that will drive revenue. Remember that "stages" come in many shapes and contexts, and that women leaders make business magic happen on stages at conferences, in board rooms and in media interviews. They "wow" stakeholders at sales pitch meetings and in the field with customer events. Wherever they are, they must be in the best spot possible to instantly grab their audience — heart, mind and soul. This approach helps leaders capitalize on snap decisions to control the conversations and the outcomes.

It's time to change the way you get dressed every morning, empowering yourself to be recognized and positioning yourself to achieve more. Embrace your "first three steps" — the actual, physical movement of your body into a room, onto a stage or into a stakeholder's line of sight. And nailing the impression you make in those first three steps comes down to three key principles. It starts from the inside out and is built upon:

1. The Story
2. The Style
3. The Brand

Every morning starts with one simple question: "What is my story today?" Here is how this comes to life with my clients.

Start with the Story

When I first meet a new client, my goal is to understand who she is as a person and as a leader. You can learn a lot by sitting down one-on-one with people and having raw and real conversations. But in Corporate America, vulnerability is hard and getting to the essence of someone and their story is even harder.

So, when I first sit down with a client, I ask a lot of questions. I need to know the answers to these questions so I can ensure that the story she lives is the story she portrays:

- What do you do outside of the office? Do you have a family or like to travel?
- What's important to you? What are your values, goals and vision?
- What are your fears? What holds you back?
- What do you do for work? What is your role within the company? What do you love about it? If you manage a team, who do you lead and how do you lead?
- What products or services does your company provide? Do you believe in the products and services?

One of the most effective ways I've found to confirm my understanding of someone is to meet with my client, then meet with their team and then validate the team's observations with my client. This is a delicate dance, and the first part of getting to know some of my clients has begun as a dressing room interview.

I intentionally use the dressing room as a place to validate some of the most important information I can about my clients. It's a great opportunity to ask some of the harder questions when they are behind closed doors, away from others.

For instance, a team has told me that they love their boss because she pushes them to be the best version of themselves. I quoted this accolade back to my client and asked, "Why do you think they said this about you? How do you do it?" These stories — their stories — are where I start to understand how my clients get to where they are and why they lead the way they do.

Armed with this information, we lay a foundation upon which to construct her looks.

Build the Style

The next phase begins by learning how she builds an outfit, her current buying behavior, the venue and location of the event or meeting we are prepping for, and the demographics of the audience she will be engaging.

I always start by asking her to tell me about an outfit that she feels the most confident in. As she explains this outfit, she is inevitably walking me through her entire process of how she creates a look. From this conversation, I learn about her decision-making behavior, how she feels about her body and her comfort zone. It's one of the most fascinating parts of the entire process because *where* she starts sets the stage for the entire conversation (and it tells me a lot about her).

Some of my clients begin with a pair of shoes, others with pants, some with a dress or even a blazer. If she begins to build her look with a loose blouse, I can tell that her midsection, her arms or her chest may be an area with which she struggles to find confidence. If she starts with her shoes and has mostly flats, she may be focused on function before fashion. On the flip side, if her closet is full of heels, then she may see her most powerful self when she slips into them.

For me, I start to build my looks with clothes that cover my legs and hips. This area has shifted a lot since I became a mom and it's important everything is covered when I stand up and sit down. I use what I call the "sit test" to ensure I'm good to go. I'll pull on a pair of jeans exactly where I want them to sit and then sit down. I move around a bit like I would if I were in a conversation. Finally, I stand back up without adjusting my pants. If my pants need massive adjustment, then I know that they aren't the right fit. Adjusting and doublechecking is a hassle to avoid.

After learning about how she builds a favorite outfit, I talk to my client about what colors she's drawn to and what colors she has an aversion to. I talk to her about necklines, textures and hemlines. I find out if her body runs "hot" or "cold," as that can be a large factor in choosing clothing selections. I also find out how she feels in button-downs, blazers, trousers, dresses and skirts. Does she prefer heels or flats? Loafers or sneakers?

I take the time to learn about her buying habits. Does she buy based on the trend, the designer or for comfort? Does she shop only four times a year, impulse buy for special events or pick up a few pieces every so often? What brands does she typically purchase? Does she shop online or prefer to try things on at the store? Does she buy on sale or does she want to be the first one to wear it? Answers to these questions tell me a lot about her ... and about how I can help her share her story.

Once I get to know my client more deeply, I redirect our conversation to learn more about the event she is preparing for. Will she be sitting or standing during the event, speech or sales pitch? If she is speaking, will she present on a stage or platform, and if so, will there be there stairs and how many? Will she be sharing the stage? If so, I gather information about the co-presenters. Will she be seen on a monitor? If so, how many monitors will there be and how big are they? Will she be wearing a wired mic, stuck behind a podium-mounted microphone or holding a microphone? Will she be walking around and moving from the stage down to the audience? Will her audience be only in front of her or will they have the capacity to see her from every angle? Will her event be streaming live?

I also like to learn as much as I can about the audience she will be engaging. How many will be attending the presentation, the meeting or the pitch? What are the ages of those in attendance? Is the audience mostly executives and decision makers, or are they managers who will bring the product or services back to their company for review? Will there be an international presence?

The more information I can filter from her, the better I can assist. When I fully understand her story and her current style, I can help her create the best version of herself to compliment her audience, product and venue location. In fact, by understanding her so well, I can help create a look that will immediately build trust with her audience within her first three steps.

When I fully understand her story and her current style, I can help her create the best version of herself to compliment her audience, product and venue location.

Every detail matters. If she will be standing for an extended period, I want to ensure she is wearing comfortable shoes. If she will be sitting, I want to assess the bottom of her shoes so that she looks put together when her shoe soles are visible, and I want to ensure that the fabric she is wearing doesn't easily wrinkle. We also need to consider socks or hosiery as well. If she will be wearing a lavalier mic, I want to ensure she is wearing something that will easily hide the wires so that they aren't distracting to her or the audience. If she will be under bright lights, it's important that her outfit isn't see-through, and I don't want her to wear a color or pattern that clashes with the stage's background. If she uses her arms when speaking, I want to ensure that her sleeves aren't restrictive, and if she is prone to sweating, I want to ensure she wears a loose top where this tendency won't be visible.

Launch the Brand

From there, I help my client focus on selecting pieces that make up the perfect outfit and that ultimately drive her confidence. The complete appearance and comfort that my client gets through this process elevates her personal brand and, in return, helps her company's brand shine as well. The experience goes beyond the clothes and accessories. It's the change of mindset each client experiences and how it makes her feel that is all the difference. This mindset shift and confidence boost is what causes a change in how she is seen by her colleagues and audience. When it all comes together, from the story to the style to the brand, everyone wins — including my client and the company she is representing.

"Know your personal brand and live by it every day - in the board meetings, presentations, conference and social posts. Be consistent, bold and, above else, authentic."

— Lynn Vojvodich, Member of the Board of Directors at Dell, Ford, Booking Holdings and Looker; Advisor and Investor in Technology Companies; Former Tech Sector CMO

Many companies are providing more training and executive coaching for their female leaders. But as I've seen up close and personal through my business experience, simply having the opportunity to be in the room or at the table isn't always enough. Women need to feel empowered and feel encouraged to have a voice. They need to own their stories and hold their brand strong.

CHAPTER 9

A Company's Biggest Asset

Many executives forget to invest in what really creates their brand: their people. In a new era when brand success depends on an organization's ability to establish trust and loyalty from its consumers, this kind of investment has become a missing link in brand development because it requires vulnerability and, let's face it, most executives are conditioned to exude confidence (not vulnerability) at all times.

Investing in the personal brands of our executive women in leadership is the most powerful tool to increase ROI and, ultimately, employee and customer loyalty by establishing trust with her and, by extension, the brand.

Think about the women who carry your company's message to the marketplace — perhaps they're C-level leaders, subject-matter experts or marketing and sales leaders. Perhaps you are the key female figurehead of your organization or one of several women who represent your brand in front of customers, influencers and the media. Media coaching and narrative development can completely prepare you to deliver a flawless, on-message interview, but how you appear — including what you wear — is the first step and, arguably, the most critical step to success.

Marketing, at its core, is simply about storytelling. It's the ability to take consumers on an emotional journey that can relate to their needs and wants while, at the same time, establishing trust in the products and services that are being provided. Trust is an emotional response, and storytelling is the most essential element in establishing it.

Storytelling through fashion is a special kind of magic.

Sell to Women, Increase Your Bottom Line

To be successful with the most powerful consumers in the world, a company must give their products and services a story that women can relate to. They must create a brand that women will buy from, advocate for and remain loyal to. Female consumers are the biggest influencers in a company's successful return on investment.

"Women are a compass for how the market is changing... We must upgrade our customer experiences to stay relevant. In a consumer economy dominated by women, new skills are needed."

- Bridget Brennan

The answer is in the ability to create an emotional connection between the information companies are sharing and the audience they are trying to reach. Consumers are the masters of snap decisions and women are master consumers, so connection — the kind that instills trust and confidence — must happen with women in an instant. Time and again, I've seen those instant connections be made by savvy executive women who understand how to use their own personal style to establish true alignment of brand and storytelling. In the end, this secret formula gives women leaders the ability to capitalize on what matters most: Trust.

Consumers are the masters of snap decisions and women are master consumers, so connection – the kind that instills trust and confidence – must happen with women in an instant.

Case Study: Her First Three Steps

Throughout this book, I have shared many stories about my clients, the largest of which has been Salesforce, with whom I have had the privilege to work and help elevate the brands of some of their most important leaders. The journey of one trailblazing woman executive at Salesforce illustrates what is possible when a global company shifts their mindset and embraces the opportunity to create an inclusive customer experience that inspires increased sales, referrals and repeat business.

Wearables That Fit

In 2016, Stephanie Buscemi was the Executive Vice President of Product and Solutions Marketing at Salesforce. She was part of the initial Dreamforce Pilot project with JD. Her assignment was to showcase Fitbit on stage during the conference. Fitbit was a marquee customer of Salesforce, and Stephanie was expected to tell their success story on stage. She and I had just met, and aligning her brand with the Fitbit brand was critical to my success.

My first step was getting to know her and her personal story. We were on a time crunch, so it was important that I authentically and quickly understood her as we prepared for the event.

Stephanie is a native of the Bay Area and a fellow UCLA alumna. She travels often and globally and gives presentations and interviews across all social media platforms. She is a dedicated mentor and leader both in and out of the office. Quick-witted, sharp and kind, Stephanie is described by her team as "the real deal." She is a powerhouse in the boardroom and commands the stage with poise, confidence and authenticity. Her natural style is "House of Cards" (Robin Wright) meets "Celine" (luxury designer).

We ended up styling Stephanie in a dress that gelled with her story and leadership style. Her outfit portrayed her as a bold, confident and sleek powerhouse.

Three Stripes Down the Side

For Dreamforce 2017, Stephanie had been promoted to Executive Vice President of Product Marketing. She was charged with announcing and presenting a huge new collaboration with Adidas. The product she highlighted was giving the consumers the ability to personalize their shoes within the Adidas app.

Building upon what I knew about Stephanie's story and leadership style, I started by understanding the product — what it did and who in the audience would use it. I then focused on the brand alignment of Stephanie, Adidas and Salesforce with intention and authenticity.

The word "personalization" was what I continued to contemplate as we worked to find her a look. It was hard. Salesforce and Adidas had styled the entire event staff with sneakers. They even customized a one-of-a-kind pair for Marc Benioff, which was shared during the keynote.

The struggle for me was finding a way to merge it all together. My gut knew that sneakers weren't going to work for Stephanie. One of her most confident pieces to wear are heels. She's petite, and I honestly don't think I've ever seen her give a presentation without them. The steps to the presentation stage would be likely higher than the standard stairs she climbed every day. She couldn't stumble, trip or look uncomfortable.

I knew Stephanie was destined to walk up three over-sized steps and onto a stage in front of an audience who will have a 360-degree view of her. She needed to drive the concept of "customization" home to the audience while wearing those three famous Adidas stripes.

Saying I was stressed would have been an

understatement. This outfit came down to the wire. Three hours before Stephanie went on stage, we decided to take a big chance. It was a massive risk for JD, but I knew that if what I had planned for her worked, the payoff would be huge.

With an audience full of Millennial women and the CEO of Adidas, I knew that her look had to be relatable and needed to be something others could buy without breaking a budget. Knowing her story, I knew heels were a confidence-driver. The sneakers everyone else was wearing wouldn't work here, but yet we couldn't ignore the brand.

In the dressing room backstage, we took a $60 dress and a $60 pencil skirt from Adidas and cut them up. I knew Stephanie liked cap sleeves for ease of movement, and she has great arms for it! And we need to integrate her signature heels into the look. She needed to look like herself — sporty and sleek. With three stripes down her sides and Celine sling-back heels, she took the stage and crushed it.

In the two minutes she was onstage, the Adidas website blew up. Everyone was looking for her look, but little did they know it was extremely one-of-a-kind. At JD, we refer to her look as the "customized Buscemi." We wanted her to have an outfit that did not distract, but rather enhanced her personality and her narrative. We started with her story, built her style and launched her brand. She successfully aligned her messaging with Salesforce and Adidas.

The Launch of a New Brand

At Dreamforce 2018, the pressure on JD amped up tenfold. Stephanie had now been promoted to Chief Marketing Officer and would be taking the stage for the first time since her promotion. Our messaging goal was to engage and inspire every member of that audience to say: "She got there. You can get there. Come with us."

We had to execute her ensemble based upon of the success of Fitbit and the huge return on the Adidas "customized Buscemi." If we wanted to have the most extreme impact on her audience, her look had to be a surprise. It felt like the Oscar Winner card or an Apple Product announcement. Her look had to be kept under lock and key until the very last second.

The brand she was showcasing that year was Ben & Jerry's. They have amazing ice cream and an amazing company, but tie-dye had no place in this look. Stephanie's new title, her story and her journey could say more and do more for the brand without showing the Ben & Jerry's logo or their bright colors.

The buzz was growing as Dreamforce neared, and everyone was curious what she would be wearing at this year's conference. Our

team at Neiman Marcus understood that we didn't want other women to see Stephanie on the stage and say, "Oh, I have that dress!" So they pulled the Celine dress we had chosen for her off the floor at the department store until she walked onto the stage. When she spoke her first words, the dress reappeared on the floor, ready to buy.

Stephanie had taken on one of the biggest CMO roles in technology. The way we defined her success this year did not come down to the hits on a website, but rather it was about validating her brand as one of Salesforce's most powerful assets. She was now in a position to hold an even greater influence — especially over all the women in the audience. Her presence on stage needed to give these women permission to dream big. With this look, Stephanie was authentic, relatable and inspiring.

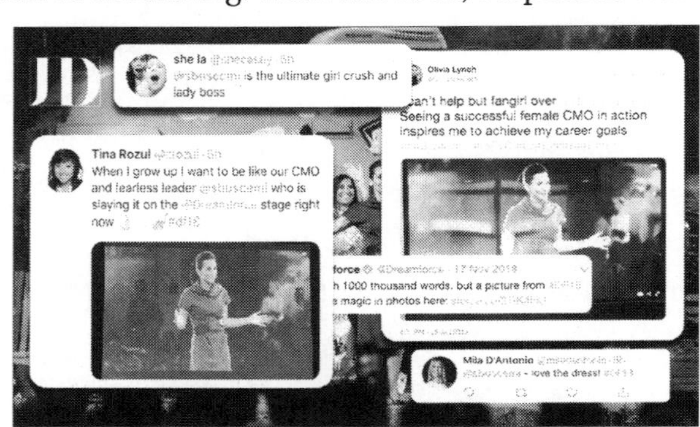

In all, one woman embraced one brand in three years with three styles. And she never neglected her one story.

As for me, I watched her walk down those stairs to exit the stage and, as she descended each step, I felt more and more exhausted.

Behind the Scenes: Walking Away

Locking the door on dressing room #2 backstage at Dreamforce for the last time, I felt a wave hit me. Still riding the adrenaline high from another incredible Dreamforce, I seemed unusually exhausted physically and fatigued mentally. I even questioned whether I could do this again. I'd barely seen my family in two months, needed to sleep for at least three days and couldn't remember the last time I had eaten a decent meal. I was too exhausted and drained to even grasp the magnitude of the moment.

I was completely burned out.

In addition to my work with Dreamforce, I was in the middle of building a product, working with a publishing agency, traveling to New York, taking on new clients and growing my team. Everything seemed important and essential to the progress of the company. My "FOMO" (not "fear of missing out" but "fear of missed opportunities") was so overwhelming that, eventually, it took a phone call from my therapist to force me to press the pause button. So, I closed the laptop, shut down new projects, stopped the product build and put hiring on hold until the new year. I spent time with the family, ate healthy, enjoyed the holidays, reconnected with friends and slept ... a lot.

Stepping away temporarily was the best thing I could have done for myself and for the company. It gave me clarity. It was a chance to reset my strategy with a fresh outlook and excitement that I hadn't felt in a long time. In fact, I discovered that some of those big projects that felt right two months prior weren't right for the business after all. Until I took time to rest and reassess, I couldn't tell the difference between what *seemed* important versus what was truly critical. And I hadn't been able to see, until I took a break, that I can't and shouldn't run a business and launch a product company at the same time.

Stepping away temporarily was the best thing I could have done for myself and for the company.

Part of my break allowed me to celebrate and reflect on the wins I did have. My head was down for so long — trying to learn markets, to network, to build a client base and to capture the corporate market - that I never took a look at how far I had come, the impact I had made and where my work was being seen.

I learned how to step back more often and appreciate what I have accomplished ... to give myself kudos for the success of my hard work. And there were plenty to celebrate:

- I had been hired by and/or partnered with 15 corporate clients, both within the retail and technology space.
- I had collaborated with two global corporations on products, services, wearables, manufacturing, technology and social media.
- I had built five key partnerships with national retail stores.
- I had hosted more than 25 private styling events in San Francisco, Los Angeles, Chicago, New York and Dallas.

- I was showcased in 15 panel talks, speaking opportunities, style contributor features and multimedia interviews.
- I worked with 45 clients across the country.
- I rebranded my company three times.

Every entrepreneur needs to find their own rhythm and balance, and for me, permission to take a break saved my company. The hiatus allowed me the time to refocus, re-energize and realize that it was time to share my story. All of it.

Every entrepreneur needs to find their own rhythm and balance, and for me, permission to take a break saved my company.

Starting from that day, in 1980, when I learned just how strong a woman can be.

ACKNOWLEDGMENTS

Writing this book was among the most challenging and rewarding experiences of my life. I owe a great deal to many people and know that my success is only possible because of them.

This book would never have been started without Dr. Barbara Smith, who believed that my stories needed to be shared. She encouraged me to put a pen in my hand and write it down and continues to listen to *all* my stories, even the ones that will never make it into a book.

I have been lucky enough to have mentors and friends of incredible ability, each of whom ensured that I had access to opportunities I simply didn't think I deserved. They include: Lauren Bernard, Katie Lass, KR Liu, Susan St. Ledger, Dan Darcy, Suzanne DiBianca, Allie Cefalo, Sylvia Borek, Rosie Cruz, Leslie Fine, Jeff Hyman, Kelly Ryan, Heather Gallagher, and Amanda Bonnell. They challenged me to think bigger and recognized in me a potential that I couldn't see.

Building a company can't be done single-handedly and I have been blessed by a group of women who gave me their time and talent, whether I could afford them or not: Carol Erdie, Paula Edmondson, Natalie Ong, Kelly Burns, Mandy Rivas, Jasmine, Diana Whitcomb, Julie Hogan, Joanne Choi and Sara Shamy.

I owe so much to Maggie Gray for taking the biggest leap of faith and riding the JD journey all the way. She consistently challenges me to think outside the box, reminds me that all stories matter and that JD's success isn't just about inspiring many but about empowering all — *one* woman at a time. Grateful, I am.

I am humbled by my generous endorsers, who took the time to read this book in its early stages and to lend their words about its strengths: Andy Cunningham, Lynn Vojvodich, Shilpa Shah, Shannon Brayton, Todd Sieling, Tylor Sherman, Ebony Frelix Beckwith, Susan St. Ledger, Suzanne DiBianca, Jessica S. Eker, Elizabeth Walton Egan, Allie Cefalo, Michael Sherlock, Cathy Fyock, Sylvia Borek, Joanne Choi and Brenna Nichols.

I have been fortunate to have women in my life who I consider more sister than friend, like Janae Corley, Lynn Lanyon, Sara Gries, Cindy Benes, Ana Vega, Lisa Hormuth, Brenna Nichols and Erin Okonek. These women supported my endeavors, showed up during the toughest of times and love my family as their own.

It is with pure gratitude to each and every one of my clients that I say "thank you" for being vulnerable and allowing me to be a part of new chapters in your lives. Each story you shared, with honesty and pure rawness, has left me inspired to continue doing what I do.

The entire team at Silver Tree Publishing deserves tremendous credit. Kate Colbert, who saw my potential as an author, helped me fine-tune what the book would accomplish and showed patience to let me finish on my own terms. Penny Tate, who gave constant support and generous timelines to make this journey as easy and fun as possible. Courtney Hudson, who brought my vision for the book cover to life. Stephanie Feger, who jumped in with a burst of energy to guide me in rebranding myself as an author and speaker. And Hilary Jastram, who showed me how to put my stories onto paper. For all the work these women did on my behalf, I am grateful.

A special thanks to Carol Erdie Photography for capturing so many events.

My family has always been a deep source of love and stability in my life. I am fortunate to have had their participation while writing the book and their willingness to talk about memories that, at times, were difficult and painful. My brother, Jonathan, is the glue that keeps our family together and a true "big brother" in every way. Writing about my childhood meant that I would be writing about his. So it is with tremendous responsibility, with his permission, that I am able to share it with you.

Trying to describe my father, Lonny, continues to be one of the hardest things for me to do. Selfless, humble, courageous, resilient, funny, compassionate and full of life — he gave up everything for his children and his family. As a father, he instilled in me that a woman can be anything she wants and that she deserves to be respected for her intelligence, grit and drive above all else. As a husband, he has stood by my mother's side for more than 50 years — unwavering in his commitment to his one-and-only love.

I must give credit to my dad for the first chapter of this book. Many hours were spent on my couch, listening to him recount traumatic and heart-wrenching memories of Mom's illness. For the first time, I was able to see just how hard it must have been for him. For the first time, I was looking back on my childhood as a mother and wife. May this book be a tribute to the life he worked so hard to give us.

My two sons, Johnathan and Evan, are the greatest achievements of my life. When I decided to write about my childhood and the times that I have struggled, it was with great awareness that my story will be a part of theirs. I am so proud of the young men they are growing up to be. Both are compassionate, open-minded and resilient. It is my hope that they will fail often, pick themselves back up, try again and find success in what they are most passionate about.

Lastly, but most importantly, my husband Dave, who read every single word of my manuscript dozens of times, allowed me to share our story, and kept pushing me to the finish line. So much of the credit for both the book and the life that I have belongs to him. Dave, marrying you was the greatest decision of my life.

GO BEYOND THE BOOK

Ready to take what you've learned in *Story. Style. Brand.* and apply it to your company or career?

Count on Janel Dyan for:

- Brand & Style Advisory Services for Organizations and Individual Leaders
- Women's Empowerment and Executive Styling Workshops
- Speaking Engagements, Podcasts and Media Appearances
- And more ...

Contact or follow Janel today:

Janel@JanelDyan.com

Instagram.com/Janel_Dyan

LinkedIn.com/in/JanelDyan

Twitter.com/Janel_Dyan

Facebook.com/JanelDyan

www.JanelDyan.com

www.StoryStyleBrand.com

ABOUT THE AUTHOR

Photo by Dan Bigelow Photography

Janel Dyan is a sought-after brand advisor to high-visibility clients across industries, politics and social causes, and founder of the firm that is best known simply as JD. She is a well-regarded expert on how to build a story to achieve brand alignment for both company and client success, and her work is seen by millions through the public appearances of Fortune 500 companies, United Nations and World Economic Forums members, technology executives and leaders in social change.

Capitalizing on our human behavior and the universal "snap decisions" we unconsciously make, Janel developed the **JD Methodology**. It is a proven method that provides corporations and individuals the ability to establish a brand that begins with trust, and a method that gives us the ability to control the conversation by asking not "what to wear" but "what story do I want to tell?"

Janel recognized early on that clothes can carry memories beyond a woman's own closet. Establishing **Beyond Us**, Janel provides opportunities to build confidence in women who need it most through a platform for the women of JD to share their clothes, and the stories they tell, with other women who are ready to take the next step in their careers or lives.

Born and raised in the San Francisco Bay Area, Janel spent more than 10 years as an organizational development consultant for technology and entertainment companies before discovering her love for brand storytelling and fashion. She is graduate of UCLA, has lived and worked in New York City, Chicago and Los Angeles, and currently resides back in the Bay with her husband and their two sons.

Made in the USA
Lexington, KY
27 November 2019

57755044R00111